NAMING RIGHTS

NAMING RIGHTS

Legacy Gifts and Corporate Money

TERRY BURTON

John Wiley & Sons, Inc.

Library of Congress Cataloging-in-Publication Data:

Burton, Terry.
    Naming rights: legacy gifts and corporate money/Terry Burton.
    p. cm.
    Includes index.
    ISBN 978-0-470-23063-3 (cloth)
    1. Institutional advertising.   2. Nonprofit organizations.   3. Fund raising.
4. Corporate image.   I. Title.
HD59.B855 2008
658.15′224–dc22

                                                        2007050509

Printed in the United States of America

10 9 8 7 6 5 4 3 2 1

To my daughters Alison and Sacia
who inspired me,
my wife Susan who believed in me,
and the fundraiser community
that makes a difference everyday.

Contents

About the Author

Terry Burton is the President and Founder of Dig In Research 2007 Inc., a fundraising research and consulting firm that assists nonprofit organizations in defining their inventory of named properties and setting the ask amounts for naming rights. For the last three years he has been conducting a national survey of naming opportunities and named gifts and uses this data to help establish the benchmarks for his clients. He is the author of three books on stewardship and donor relations, co-author to fundraising research in Canada on corporate giving, employee giving in the workplace, foundation giving and sponsorships. In 1995, he helped to design PRO—Prospect Research Online, the first online resource to provide in-depth information about corporate philanthropy, details about officers and directors and related information that have strategic importance in qualifying and identifying funding prospects. Burton has also published more than a dozen articles for supportingadvancement.com, Ezines.com, CASE *Currents* magazine, and *Canadian Fundraiser*. He is a frequent speaker on naming rights at conferences and seminars (APRA National Conference, AHP, AFP National and local chapter events), and he lives in Vancouver, British Columbia.

Introduction

When someone mentions naming rights these days, you can't help but notice the reaction from others in the room. It seems as though a week doesn't pass without a major news story telling the tale of another named gift or other naming rights deal. Naming rights have emerged as a hot topic for discussion and taken on strategic importance for fundraisers.

As with most things in life, you have to give something of significance if you want to get something significant in return. The commodity of choice for nonprofits has become naming rights to their tangible properties and endowment funds. "Cash is king," so the business saying goes, and fundraising leaders haven't ignored the lesson. A named gift or sponsorship can be worth millions of dollars. As a result, naming rights have become an integral part of fundraising plans, whether a nonprofit is in or out of a campaign.

The use of giving or naming opportunities in a fundraising campaign was once deemed to be reserved for the upper echelon of nonprofit entities. Now, however, the tactic has spread throughout the sector. A growing number of nonprofits, municipalities, and other groups are willing to grant naming rights in exchange for financial considerations. From conservation groups to the Salvation Army, from school districts and private schools to YM/YWCAs, fundraising campaigns include the offer of naming rights for tangible and intangible assets of all shapes and sizes.

And the practice is growing fast. In 1997, only two universities in the United States were in the midst of billion-dollar fundraising drives. As of December 2007, there were more than 30. Each one of those campaigns features a wide assortment of giving or naming opportunities for prospective donors, ranging from naming a campus or a college to naming a scholarship endowment fund. With naming gifts available for prices ranging from thousands of dollars to millions, naming/giving opportunities have become the commodities of choice in the current era. And although traditionally these naming rights were transferred to an individual, private foundation, corporation, or other benefactor in perpetuity, that, too, is changing.

Giving or naming opportunities (the terms are used interchangeably) and their price tags are the topics I will examine with you. This book is written for professional fundraising staff in nonprofit organizations who live in a world where the competition for the fundraising dollar has become more intense. As the dollar amounts of the campaigns creep ever higher, the nature of the ask for a major gift has changed to one that is based more on the relationship between donor and recipient than on modest direct mail solicitations that seek to evoke an emotional response.

WHAT PRICE FOR NAMING RIGHTS?

Over the last several years, I have been conducting *The National Survey of Naming Opportunities and Named Gifts*. To date, my research has collected more than 32,000 entries from the United States and Canada. The information was gathered by doing desktop enquiries using the Internet, conducting telephone interviews, and reviewing hard-copy campaign reports. The results suggest that the nonprofit sector often struggles with the notion of appropriate ask amounts for naming rights.

There are many similarities between completing the sale of a residential property and completing the negotiation of a gift to a nonprofit with naming rights attached. The most important point in both scenarios is setting the asking price.

How much should you ask to name a building or an endowment? That has become the million-dollar question. The properties owned by nonprofits, commonly referred to as *naming opportunities*, can be worth millions of dollars. Publishing an appropriate ask amount that reflects the current market conditions for a designated asset can be the difference between "making the sale," as they say in the real estate business, or having your property stay on the market.

Allow me to share a story with you. Last summer, I was on my way to Chicago to make a presentation on emerging trends in naming opportunities to the Association of Professional Researchers for Advancement (www.aprahome.org), an industry group made up of research staff. I was riding in an O'Hare Airport shuttle heading downtown. As I casually chatted with fellow passengers, I was asked what kind of work I do, and I said research on naming rights. I was surprised at the level of interest and passionate opinions this subject brought out in my fellow passengers. Normally, the route from O'Hare into downtown Chicago via the heavily congested expressway system seems like it takes forever, but not on this day.

No sooner had I said the words "naming rights" than one passenger jumped right in, with noted disdain in her voice, to take the moral high road on the subject of universities selling naming rights. The lady's traveling companion added her own short affirmations from time to time, acknowledging that her friend was right on the mark in her opinion. Their comments reminded me of similar words coming from the mainstream media. For the umpteenth time, I listened to what I felt were uninformed and biased opinions that naming rights were all about corporate giants coming in and compromising the integrity of an institution just so it could fatten its wallet. This went on for several minutes. She summed up her protests, stating rhetorically "... why can't we go back to the way things were before?" Talk about shooting the messenger! I felt like I had a bull's-eye on my chest.

I paused for a moment before replying. "Do you want the new library, the state-of-the-art medical school, more scholarship money for aspiring students? How about the medical equipment that will be part of that new hospital? Funding shortfalls from government are on the rise, and nonprofit organizations have looked inward to find new ways to raise the funds they need. Where else is the money going to come from?" My question did not get a reply.

I continued, "Nonprofit organizations have tangible properties that have value. Each one of these properties is a 'naming opportunity' that can be marketed by nonprofit organizations. Each naming opportunity—a hospital, a school, an area within the library—is a unique property worth money to the nonprofit entity. In appreciation for a cash gift or multiyear pledge, nonprofit institutions, a group that includes the largest universities and colleges in the country, have traditionally thanked the donor by placing the donor's name on the facility or endowment to commemorate the gift."

Naming rights come after the fact. I asked them, "Where would the money would come from, if not from the sale of naming rights? Do you think people would be willing to pay higher taxes instead?" No reply. It was a quiet ride the rest of the way into Chicago.

I remember thinking to myself that nonprofit groups, especially the well-known universities, hospitals, museums, and others that receive high-profile named gifts and sponsorships, really need to do a better job of educating the community about what they will do with the money. It's about stewardship. But we'll discuss that later in the book.

Competition is what's driving us down the road to more, better, best. And our competition is on a global scale, fostered by the increasing demands of our own up-tempo lifestyles. Education is considered one of the keys to winning the fight in the global village. The United States' aging population is retiring, with increasing numbers leaving the workforce every year. The demand on the younger generations is growing exponentially as a result. The entire education sector is racing to bring improved and increased capacity online as soon as possible to meet the demands for a better-educated workforce. As they do so, new fundraising campaigns have emerged to finance the growth that comes from replacing old and outdated facilities and expanding to meet the demand for state-of-the-art engineering, medical, and computer-related education programs that were not even in existence 10 years ago.

Funding these new facilities and offering the accompanying scholarship support takes a lot of money. Government sources and bond issues cover only so much; the rest has to come from private sources. This is where we can see how the naming opportunities fit into the nonprofit fundraising plan. Nonprofits can sell the naming rights to physical properties that can be seen and touched, as well as to endowments gifts, to get the funds they need to accomplish their goals. But every now and then, a surprise benefactor comes along and makes a transformational gift.

A NONPROFIT NAMED GIFT: LIKE WINNING THE LOTTERY

As you read these pages, consider this notion: Landing a top-of-the-pile naming rights deal for a nonprofit organization is better than winning the lottery. Really! Six-, seven-, eight- and nine-figure naming gifts have a transformational impact on nonprofit organizations.

Every time an organization signs a naming rights deal, that organization is forever transformed by the impact of the amount of money now at their disposal. Making an ask for a large philanthropic gift or sponsorship is never a sure thing. The best intentions of a would-be donor have been known not to materialize into an actual gift for any number of reasons or unexpected events. So on the day a big check arrives at the nonprofit's door, there is cause for celebration. Many of the gifts large enough to earn naming rights often help elevate the operational effectiveness of the organization. It's better than winning the lottery in a random draw of chance. Effectively, a large monetary gift means that someone stepped up and said "Yes, I believe in what you are doing and what you are going to do with my money. Here is my check."

For the nonprofit's staff, the naming rights gift is a validation for the hard work they have done and plan to do in the future. It's an indirect vote of confidence that helps fuel morale for the ongoing mission and the vision of the organization as a whole.

At times they get to pay off debt, sometimes all of it. They get to build new buildings, expand the delivery of programs and services, and push forward in their efforts to serve the greater good. And unlike lottery winners in many countries, they don't have to pay taxes on the newfound money.

Putting naming rights on the market has become an easy decision. It's so commonplace these days that the marketplace for these commodities is extending to previously unheard-of naming opportunities.

PRIVATE SECTOR BOUNTY

In the private sector, investors can compare naming rights between one venue and the next by developing an apples-to-apples comparison. Generally, you are provided with the statistics for a venue such as a stadium or arena; you can examine the demographics regarding who attends events and with what frequency. Blend the number of events and the estimated swirl in the projected number of bottoms in seats for those events, and you can identify what I call the Class One candidates for brand name publicity.

One other factor has an enormous impact on the market value of naming rights. As real estate agents have so often said about residential property, "location, location, location" is the number one factor is determining the market value of a property. And so it is with naming rights as well.

MAKING USE OF THIS INFORMATION

Think of this book as a portable Manager's Toolbox on naming rights. As we examine recent events, we can see that the tide is turning towards a broader acceptance of the private sector model for naming rights and the creation of a new realm within the nonprofit sector.

For the most part, the nonprofit sector looks at naming rights and naming opportunities through a different lens than the private sector. In the pages of this book, we will examine naming rights from these two distinctly different, yet somewhat similar, points of view. We will look at private sector naming rights from megadeals for professional sports venues to local examples that exemplify corporate partnership. At the other end of the spectrum, we'll examine contemporary snapshots of the nonprofit sector, including universities, colleges, hospitals, museums, environmental groups, and a wide assortment of other organizations.

When you have turned the last page, I hope to have shared with you insights and perspectives that clarify the issues, answer your questions, and urge you to learn more.

~ 1 ~

Escalating Price Tags For High-Profile Properties

Let's set the stage for our discussion of naming rights by examining one of the most significant trends in the marketplace: escalating price tags for high-profile properties. This is one of the top three trends I see that is having the greatest impact on the nonprofit sector as mentioned in my presentation to the AFP National Conference of Philanthropy, 2008 in San Diego and part of my PowerPoint presentation available online at the Web site www.supportingadvancement.com.

There are two distinct sectors offering marquee properties: the private sector and the nonprofit sector. They are linked at the hip, so to speak, both by association with naming rights and by the market forces at work today. Supply and demand, the most fundamental of economic theories, appear to be at the center of any discussion of what price tag to place on naming opportunities. As you look around at your own organization and those of your peers, you'll find that there is a limited supply of high-profile properties available today.

Why is that? Historical choices made in years gone by limit the availability of high-profile properties today, because traditionally, naming rights were granted in perpetuity. If we use a university campus as our example, there is only one school of medicine, one school of business, engineering, law, etc. The supply is limited, and once a naming gift has been received, each one of those named high-profile properties is off the market.

One of the most curious aspects about naming rights and the trends I have seen in the market is that naming activity seems to have peaks and valleys. A key attribute within this trend is the sharp upward spike in the dollar value of the named gifts received.

HIGH-PROFILE NAMING OPPORTUNITIES IN THE NONPROFIT SECTOR

Named Schools of Business

A lot of variables go into the formula for establishing the asking price of high-value properties, such as a school of business. Take a look at Exhibit 1.1, which lists the dollar value and the year of naming gifts to universities during the 1990s.

Of the 80 named business schools in my survey, 37 (46%) were named with a private gift (i.e., the donor asked the institution not to reveal the

EXHIBIT 1.1 Named Business Schools in the 1990s

University of Southern California—Marshall School of Business (1997) Los Angeles, CA	$35 million
University of Iowa—Tippie College of Business (1999) Iowa City, IA	$30 million
New York University—Stern School of Business (1988) New York, NY	$30 million
University of South Carolina—Moore School of Business (1998) Columbia, SC	$25 million
Indiana University—Kelley School of Business (1997) Bloomington, IN	$23 million
University of Denver—Daniels College of Business (1999) Denver, CO	$22 million
University of Oklahoma—Price College of Business (1997) Tulsa, OK	$18 million
University of Kentucky—Gatton College of Business and Economics (1996) Lexington, KY	$17 million
University of Maryland—Smith School of Business (1998) College Park, MD	$15 million
University of Alabama—Culverhouse College of Commerce and Business Administration (1998) Tuscaloosa, AL	$14.5 million
Georgia State University—Robinson College of Business (1997) Atlanta, GA	$10 million
Bradley University—Foster College of Business (1994) Peoria, IL	$7.5 million

Source: Dig In Research 2007 Inc., *National Survey of Naming Opportunities*

dollar amount of the gift). That means we know the dollar amount of the naming gift for 63% of the 80 business schools. Most would agree this is a representative sample from which we can draw conclusions and make fairly accurate predictions.

Exhibit 1.2 lists the business schools named since the year 2000. You will notice a dramatic jump in the dollar values of the named gifts received. It is worth noting the distribution of which schools landed naming gifts, sometimes less than 10 years later than their peer institutions. The upward shifting trends suggest many things, including how the perceived value of a named school has changed so dramatically over the last decade.

EXHIBIT 1.2 Named Business Schools since 2000

Stanford University—Knight Management Center (2006) Palo Alto, CA	$105 million
University of Michigan—Ross School of Business (2004) Ann Arbor, MI	$100 million
University of Wisconsin at Madison—School of Business to remain un named for 20 years (2007) Madison, WI	$85 million
Carnegie Mellon University—Tepper School of Business (2004) Pittsburgh, PA	$55 million
University of Washington, Seattle—Foster School of Business (2007) Seattle, WA	$50 million
Johns Hopkins University—Carey Business School (2006) Baltimore, OH	$50 million

University of Texas at Austin—McCombs School of Business (2000) Austin, TX	$50 million
University of Houston—Bauer College of Business (2000) Houston, TX	$40 million
University of Tampa—Sykes College of Business (2000) Tampa, FL	$38 million
University of Colorado—Leeds School of Business (2001) Denver, CO	$35 million
College of William and Mary—Mason School of Business (2005) Williamsburg, VA	$30 million
University of California, Irvine—Merage School of Business (2005) Irvine, CA	$30 million
Northern Arizona University—Franke College of Business (2007) Flagstaff, AZ	$25 million
University of Hawaii—Shidler College of Business (2006) Honolulu, HI	$25 million
St. Mary's University—Greehey School of Business (2005) San Antonio, TX.	$25 million
California State University, Fullerton—Mihaylo College of Business and Economics (2008) Fullerton, CA	$30 million
Ball State University—Miller College of Business (2003) Muncie, IN	$17 million
University of Washington, Tacoma—Milgard School of Business (2007) Tacoma, WA	$15 million

(Continued)

EXHIBIT 1.2 (Continued)

Texas A&M Universtity—Mays Business School (2005) College Station, TX	$15 million
University of Wisconsin, Milwaukee—Lubar School of Business (2006) Milwaukee, WI	$10 million
Rowan University—Rohrer College of Business (2005) Glassboro, NJ	$10 million

Source: Dig In Research 2007 Inc., *National Survey of Naming Opportunities*

Wow! What a difference a decade can make! That's 21 named schools of business since the year 2000. The last six entries would have ranked highly among named gifts just 10 years earlier.

As the years go by, the supply of high-profile properties—in this case, schools of business—has been diminishing, which has helped to drive up the asking amount to name the schools. Except for one university, just one.

BUSINESS SCHOOL TO GO UNNAMED FOR 20 YEARS AFTER $85 MILLION GIFT

What's in a name? Interesting question these days, especially in the higher education sector.

On Friday, October 26th, the University of Wisconsin, Madison announced a most unusual gift to its Business School. It seems that a number of alumni had gotten together to make a group gift to the school.

That's not too unusual these days as class gifts and other informal groups have banded together to support a common interest. With this group of UW–Madison supporters, the minimum buy-in was a no-nonsense $5 million commitment. They call themselves the Wisconsin Naming Partnership. The gift they made to the university was $85 million.

In today's marketplace $85 million buys you some latitude with regard to naming rights. That was precisely what the Wisconsin Naming Partnership wanted. Their gift came with one caveat, that the School of Business shall go unnamed for a single donor or entity for the next 20 years. In the big scheme of things, this gift of $85 million ranks #3 all time in publicly announced gifts to a school of business.

According to my research, over 80 Schools/ Colleges of Business have been named across the USA dating back to 1881 when the University of Pennsylvania named the Wharton School of Business for a private gift. Over the years many other universities have also received private gifts to name the business school including MIT, Notre Dame, University of Arkansas and Dartmouth College.

There are a lot of ways we can look at this event. On the one hand we have a committed group of alumni with a passion for their school of business and the financial means to support it. As individuals no one member of the group could have pulled this off, but together they were able to do what many would have said was impossible.

Pooling their resources together to collect $85 million was a remarkable feat unto itself. Requesting that their business school remain unnamed for the next twenty years is unprecedented. It's interesting to note that the request was not to leave the school of business unnamed in perpetuity, something the group could have asked for given the dollar amount of their gift.

Twenty years from now the University of Wisconsin—Madison will have a renewable asset coming of age. Perhaps then there will be a naming donor, or fast forward twenty years and see that the tradition established in 2007 is something so unique and revered by the university, alumni, and friends that a second Wisconsin Naming Partnership group is formed to continue what began today. An interesting pivot and turn in the grand scheme of things don't you think?

How many others will follow the lead of the University of Wisconsin–Madison and have unnamed schools for a limited time contract period? How many other donors will shift to the contrarian path and make an unnamed gift to a university, college, hospital, museum or other favorite charity just because they can?

The large anonymous gift is not unheard of. On May 30, 2007, the University of Chicago announced an anonymous $100-million gift from an alumnus who preferred to avoid the spotlight and not have his (or her) name revealed, nor receive any sort of named recognition. The magnanimous gift was directed towards undergraduate student aid and announced by the university's president, Robert Zimmer, to kick off a $400 million campaign. The joy comes in the giving.

In Erie, Pennsylvania, a town of 100,000 that has struggled since the closure of the iron and steel plants in the community, Christmas came early on

November 13, 2007. Some 46 charities met that day at the offices of the Erie Community Foundation to hear the news of an anonymous gift of $100 million. The executive director of the Foundation, Mitch Batchelor, is sworn to secrecy and apparently answered all enquires with only a smile.

Earlier in 2007, Washington and Lee University president Kenneth Ruscio made a surprise announcement during the convocation ceremony on June 7. The liberal arts college had been given a $100-million gift, one of the largest ever made in to such a school in the United States, by an anonymous donor.

Such generosity is not just a passing fancy or whim by the recent rich. On May 7, 2001, Johns Hopkins University announced an anonymous gift of $100 million to its Bloomberg School of Public Health. The donor requested that the funds go towards developing new vaccines and drugs for malaria. At the time, this was the largest gift ever for a single purpose.

The Southwestern Medical Center at the University of Texas received a wonderful surprise late in 2003. A $50 million gift arrived from an anonymous donor for the Dallas-based group in early November to help top a $300-million fundraising campaign that was underway at the time.

These are just a few of many examples of anonymous gifts made by donors who prefer to go unnamed. At a time when universities are pressing forward with ambitious fundraising campaigns and offering their most precious commodities, naming rights to a school or college in return for a mega gift, this initiative is so unique in nature that it deserves its fifteen minutes of fame.

The University of Wisconsin–Madison's unnaming gift sent shock waves through the ranks of higher education fundraisers. I spoke with the senior development staff at one of the top 25 universities shortly after the announcement, and it was suggested that the university, the recent recipient of a large named gift, was pausing to think more about its own naming policies. It only takes one stone to send ripples through the pond.

Legacy gifts by individuals and foundations have risen substantially over the past several years. Corporations, too, are stepping up their involvement on campus with naming gifts for athletic facilities, endowments, and other facilities. Corporate dollars have been an integral part of higher education for decades, but they have traditionally been given in the sponsored-programs area, dedicated to research efforts. Corporate America has recently begun to take a closer look at how to leverage the money they give to universities and other nonprofit organizations from a brand-building point of view. With an ever-shrinking pool of pro sports venues that offer high-profile brand name marketing and business development opportunities, corporate eyes have swiveled towards the next tier down in the naming rights marketplace. We can expect to see a surge in new deals with hospitals, performing arts, museums, school boards, community colleges, and especially universities and colleges, in 2008 and beyond.

Adapted from Terry Burton's article, *Business School to go Unnamed for 20 Years After $85 Million Gift*, www.supportingadvancement.com, 2007.

How will this event impact the fundraising strategies of major universities? Will the University of Wisconsin–Madison stand alone with their unnamed school of business? Unlike other universities and colleges, which have been seeking out this type of major gift, the University of Wisconsin–Madison has a 20-year limited term on its unnamed property. All others are named in perpetuity.

At the University of Southern California, Los Angeles, 10 of the 17 undergraduate schools have received naming endowment gifts already. Neighboring Stanford University, ranked alongside USC within the top 25 universities nationally, has one named school, the Knight Graduate School of Business, as previously listed.

Schools of business are just one part of the university campus that have been the beneficiaries of naming gifts, endowments designed to not only preserve but also enhance the long-term goals of the institution.

While the deans of business schools have been rejoicing, their colleagues in the other high-profile faculties, including medicine, law, and engineering, have had their own share of champagne celebrations for naming gifts. In comparison to the business schools, there have not been as many schools of medicine named with an endowment gift—but the dollar values of the naming gifts are relatively higher, as shown in Exhibit 1.3.

That scenario is common with universities, colleges, hospitals, arts and culture organizations,

EXHIBIT 1.3 Named Schools of Medicine

University of California, Los Angeles—Geffen School of Medicine (2002) Los Angeles, CA	$200 milllion
Johns Hopkins University—Kimmel Cancer Center (2001) Baltimore, MD	$150 million
University of Southern California—Keck School of Medicine (1998) Los Angeles, CA	$110 million
McMaster University—DeGroote School of Medicine (2003) Hamilton, ON, Canada	$105 million
Brown University—Alpert Medical School (2007) Providence, RI	$100 million
University of Miami—Miller School of Medicine (2004) Miami, FL	$100 million
Cornell University—Weill Medical College (1998) Ithaca, NY	$100 million
University of Iowa—Carver School of Medicine (2002) Iowa City, IA	$90 million
Northwestern University—Feinberg School of Medicine (2002)	$75 million

Source: Dig In Research 2007 Inc., *National Survey of Naming Opportunities*

and many other nonprofits. Some people are anxious about corporate sponsorship and all that comes with it.

The top-tier universities have an alumni base that includes a generous collection of individuals with high net worth individuals. For these institutions, the corporate-named facility, especially a corporate-named school, may be a long time in coming. But for the second-, third-, and fourth-tier universities, the community colleges, the school districts, hospitals, museums and performing arts venues, corporate naming/branding gifts are beginning to take hold—not just in the United States, but in other countries as well.

Fundraising campaigns numbering in the hundreds have as their goal massive amounts of cash, as compared to those of 10 and 15 years ago. They are helping to restock the nonprofit sector with new buildings, new colleges, libraries, medical centers, and the like, each with a high-end price tag. Donors love them. More than 90% of the named gifts you see in the tables above have gone to create or build new facilities.

My research suggests that legacy gifts to charities are, at the very least, a distant cousin to the acquisition fees paid to name venues and events that promote brand names. The legacy gift makes a statement about the individual making the gift, whether it was $10 million, $50 million, $100 million, or more, and about the high net worth community as a whole. The capacity to give amongst the über-rich, as they are sometimes called, has skyrocketed in tandem with their swollen bank accounts, equity valuations, hedge fund bonanzas, and other alternative investments that have added numerous zeroes to the personal net worth of the upper class.

For both the organizations offering naming rights and the prospective philanthropic donors or corporate buyers, the upward pressure, especially on marquee properties, brings a certain amount of angst to the process. Coming up with the dollar amount for the asking price tag to name the property can be a difficult challenge, especially in a marketplace where the benchmarks are continually shifting. Choosing which organization to give the money to may be an equally difficult choice for the philanthropist.

Health Care and Escalating Naming Gifts

Hospitals, cancer centers (for patient care as well as cancer research), and other health care–related properties appear to be riding the coattails of the success of universities and colleges. The exchange of naming rights for mega-gifts of $100 million and more is evidence of the importance given to wealthy donors who want to make a difference with a hospital or health care–related gift.

Health care is on the minds of a majority of seniors, especially those of the baby boomer generation. On March 21, 2006, City of Hope in Los Angeles dedicated the Arnold and Mabel Beckman Center for Cancer Immunotherapeutics and Tumor Immunology after the couple's foundation made a $20 million gift. According to the announcement from City of Hope, the Beckmans' gift will be directed toward building an integrated research facility that will focus on tumor immunology and research on converting scientific discoveries into innovative treatments and diagnostic methodology for cancer patients.

Ten years ago, a $20 million gift would have made national headlines. In 2006, the news of this generous contribution barely made it out of California. Despite the generosity of the gift and the importance of City of Hope's efforts, in today's marketplace it take a bigger splash to get the attention of the national media. The escalating price tags and the named gifts received have raised the bar of what is a newsworthy story.

As you review Exhibit 1.4, note that Nationwide Insurance, a corporate sponsor, made a remarkable choice to give $50 million to the Children's Hospital in St. Louis, Missouri, in 2006. This gift is particularly noteworthy because it is the most significant corporate gift to a high-profile property in the nonprofit sector since Mattel's $25 million gift to UCLA's Children's Hospital in 2002.

A sign of things to come? I think so. Why? Because the number of traditional high-profile properties available for naming opportunities has shrunk dramatically. We'll discuss that further in Chapter 2.

In my three years researching this topic and twenty years doing other philanthropic research, I have come across several organizations that use innovative strategies and tactics to market their naming rights. One of the most creative online

EXHIBIT 1.4 Escalating Price Tags for Naming Rights in
              Health Care

Sanford Health System (2007) Sioux City, SD	$400 million
University of Southern California—Mann Institute for Biomedical Engineering (1998) Los Angeles, CA	$112.5 million
University of California, Davis—Moore School of Nursing (2007) Davis, CA	$100 million
Ann & Robert H. Lurie Children's Hospital (2007) Chicago, IL	$100 million
Texas Children's Hospital—Duncan Neurological Research Institute (2007) Houston, TX	$50 million
Nationwide Children's Hospital (2006) St. Louis, MO	$50 million
University of North Carolina—Gillings School of Public Health (2007) Chapel Hill, NC	$50 million
University of Texas—Southwestern Medical Center Simmons Comprehensive Center for Research and Treatment in Brain and Neurological Disorders (2008) Dallas, TX	$50 million
Dana Farber Cancer Center (2008) Shapiro Cancer Clinic Boston, MA	$27 million
Washington University in St. Louis—Wolff Institute for Biomedical Research (2008) St. Louis, MO	$20 million
University of Notre Dame—Eck Center for Global Health and Infections Disease (2008) South Bend, IN	$20 million

Source: Dig In Research 2007 Inc., *National Survey of Naming Opportunities*

marketing strategies was developed by the Children's Hospital of Atlanta (www.choa.org). The campaign that recently completed featured an innovative approach to sharing information about naming opportunities While the Web pages were available you could click on the link to "About the Foundation," and there you would have found a left-side navigation bar that included a link to "Naming Opportunities." Users interested in giving could click on a link for "Naming Opportunities," which led to a Web page that was simple, yet elegant. The usual staff contact information and phone number were available, but what came next was very cool.

The Web site visitor was invited to learn more about the naming opportunities for Children's Hospital of Atlanta's facilities and programs by specialty area classification or by price range. If you chose specialty area classification, you could view up to 18 specialty subsections of naming opportunities. Alternately, you could view the information by price range, which extended from $50,000 to $50 million to name the building addition at the Children's Hospital at Egleston.

The innovative approach of using a flat file type of database, with two choices to view the information, within the campaign Web site was very clever on the part of the fundraising team and especially the information technology support person who devised it. This kind of tactic is indicative of the changing nature of the marketplace and the ways that donor relations staff are using the organization's

Web site to keep in touch with their donor community. In a later chapter, we will go into more detail about the marketing strategies and tactics in use today.

I spoke with Jane Ellington, Director of Donor Relations for the Children's Hospital of Atlanta, and asked her about their innovative approach to naming opportunities.

"It really did serve us well," said Ellington. "We were able to go into the internal Web site and update the list while the campaign was underway. This gave us a tool to work together." She went on to remark that the foundation office did receive a number of phone calls about the naming opportunities from prospective donors. Ellington felt that the format "allowed the donors to feel like they were more involved in the decision-making process," as compared to other campaigns where the donor is typically presented with a limited selection of major gift naming opportunities.

The foundation's staff were able to make notes on individual properties, especially when a donor showed specific interest. They could add a note to the file and reserve a potential named property for up to 60 days. This is another feature that the staff found to be very helpful.

The online database was created from scratch by Robert Massey, the lead software engineer for the hospital, who was given some general directions by the foundation staff and then created the interactive naming opportunities page using the Oracle database program.

$100 MILLION NAMING RIGHTS: ENTITLEMENT OR NEED?

Mile high expectations or just a fishing trip?

In late November of 2006, the University of Colorado announced a $25 million gift from Denver philanthropist Phillip Anschutz. In appreciation of this donation, the Medical Campus in Aurora was re-named in Anschutz's honor.

The School of Medicine used the announcement to trumpet the call for a naming rights donor, asking price $100 million—an interesting tactic in the grand scheme of fundraising efforts.

An emerging trend in the nonprofit sector is the supercharged escalation of ask amounts for naming rights. This trend is directly linked to the surge in billion dollar fundraising campaigns currently underway at universities, colleges, environmental groups and others across the USA.

I wonder aloud sometimes and ask the wind, "Who checks the moral barometer of nonprofit entities?"

Which organization is genuinely qualified to ask for a $100 million gift in return for the perpetual naming rights to an intangible like a school of medicine? Is this about entitlement or need?

Trend in Named Gifts to Universities

Last August Stanford University received a $105 million gift from the founder of Knight Industries and in turn named the Knight Graduate School of Management. The dollar amount of $105 million, by the way, made it the number one ranked named gift to a business school, $5 million more than the gift made to the University of Michigan in December of 2004.

Stanford is ranked #7 Best National University—Doctoral level by the U.S. News and World Report. The six schools ahead of Stanford include Princeton, Harvard, Yale, Cal Tech, Duke and MIT.

Now add to that perspective that there are only two business schools that have received a nine-figure gift. That's it. Of the 67 named business schools, #21 ranked Carnegie Mellon University, is next, having received a $55 million gift in 2004.

For the record, there have been more naming gifts made to business schools than to medicine, law, and engineering combined. Capitalism helped to create wealth; some are giving back in a big way.

Naming rights for nonprofit organizations take their benchmarks from these named business schools. Every now and then there is a gift outside the norm, made by someone who has financial capacity and a strong emotional attachment to the institution.

UCLA—David Geffen School of Medicine (2002)	$200 million
University of Miami—Miller School of Medicine (2004)	$100 million
Cornell University—Weill Medical College (1998)	$100 million

Northwestern University—Feinburg School of Medicine (2002)	$75 million
Stanford—Knight School of Management (2006)	$105 million
University of Michigan—Ross School of Business (2004)	$100 million
Carnegie Mellon University—Tepper School of Business (2004)	$55 million
University of Texas, Austin—McCombs School of Business (2004)	$50 million

I pose the question somewhat rhetorically. Are the asking amounts for naming rights about need or are they based on some sense of entitlement?

To the universities and colleges, receiving a large naming gift is like winning the lottery. Truth be known, it's better because unlike someone who claims a windfall from a random lottery ticket, there are no state or federal withholding taxes skimmed off the top. It's more like cashing in a tax-free prize from the Irish Sweepstakes.

Twenty years ago, philanthropy was all about contributing to a favorite charity because of the emotional ties that made us a part of the organization.

Contemporary fundraisers seem to be focused in on pushing for as much as they can get every time they ask for a gift. Profiling of the would-be donors is skewed towards a what's-in-it-for-us background research according to wealth indicators. Many times the profiles are compiled without ever having a conversation with the individual, foundation, corporation, or other possible benefactor.

Maybe it's the system that is bent. When senior fundraising staff look around and see the off-the-chart numbers being asked for naming rights at other schools they appear to be ready to announce in public, "me too."

Is that enough? Who gets to pose the questions asking organizations to validate their ask amounts? Hopefully some of the donor community or perhaps a trustee.

Should they not have to back it up with some sort of track record of outstanding accomplishments such as a highly touted academic curriculum, maybe a Nobel Prize–winning faculty on staff or evidence of breakthrough research by accomplished professors? How did they come up with a $100 million price tag anyway?

Why are they not accountable to show deemed value in these naming rights? Should the donor community blindly accept any dollar amount that a university or college or any other nonprofit organizations promotes as the ask for its naming rights?

In a market economy, the theory is that the marketplace will influence the price based on the Law of Supply and Demand. Based on my observations the nonprofit sector does not always operate in lock step with the free market principles when it comes to naming rights for properties, especially the high-ticket items. Scarcity has a significant influence on what that price tag should be. I wonder how much the final decision is influenced by need or the sense of entitlement?

And what kind of influence do these high-minded tactics have on the rest of the nonprofit organizations in that community? This is not to mention the impact they have on donor's choices to distribute the same amount of money to a wider group of deserving organizations.

A month before I wrote this article there was an announcement from the corporate side of the fence. Citibank, the largest financial services company in the land and one of the largest in the world, announced two naming rights deals on successive days.

The first was a commercial sector naming rights agreement for $20 million a year for 20 years, a $400 million deal, for the new baseball stadium where the New York Mets play. The second was a $34 million dollar deal to name the Wang Center for Performing Arts in Boston.

Isn't it interesting to see a bank buying naming rights in both the private sector and nonprofit at these dollar levels? Building up brand name appears to have elevated to new heights in terms of perceived value.

Are universities and colleges that employ these aggressive fundraising strategies strictly working towards the fulfilling their role to enhance the greater good or merely acting out repressed ambitions to be the wealthiest kid on the block?

The information in this section is taken from an article that I wrote and appears at the online Web site located at www.supportingadvancement.com. That Web site has become a dynamic resource for many fundraising professionals who are in and outside of higher education.

PRIVATE SECTOR: ESCALATING PRICE TAGS

Let's look at the other side of the naming rights marketplace. Private sector companies have sought out naming opportunities to enhance and in some cases create brand name recognition, sponsorship benefits, and long-term business development opportunities. One of the most common references these days is to the naming rights of professional sports venues, so we'll start by taking a look at what's going on with the price tags for naming rights with professional sports. The high-profile nature of pro sports serves as one aspect of benchmarking the going rate for a named property in the marketplace today.

Keep in mind that there are two types of naming scenarios for pro sports facilities. On one hand, you have naming rights for a newly constructed stadium or multipurpose arena; on the other, you have naming rights for an existing venue when the previous naming rights deal has expired. The location of the venue has a lot to do with how much the owner can ask to name the venue. In New York, two naming rights deals have been concluded within the last year, at $400 million each. In contrast, the stadium in Jacksonville, Florida, where the Jaguars pro football team plays its games, may only fetch half that amount.

Marketing, media hits, and brand name exposure are all a part of the corporate naming rights game. How the numbers are determined is a mystery, with no consistent rules that apply across the board. The New Jersey Sports Authority has asked for bids to name their prized property, the Continental Airlines Arena. The naming rights expire in 2008, and the primary tenant, the NBA's New Jersey Nets, is moving to a new home. In Dallas, Texas, the owner of the Dallas Cowboys football team has reportedly asked for a billion dollars to name his stadium, which was built only a few years ago. So far, there have been no takers.

In 1920, William Wrigley, Jr., became the owner of the Chicago Cubs. He was also the president of Wrigley Gum and owned the Wrigley Building. In 1926, the ball park was renamed Wrigley Field. In his retirement years, Mr. Wrigley was heard to say that the decision to name the field after himself helped sell more gum in the city of Chicago than any other marketing effort they had ever tried.

Baseball Stadium Naming Rights

Let's take a look at major league baseball. Exhibit 1.5 lists named ball parks, ranked by the dollar value of their naming rights agreements.

EXHIBIT 1.5 Major League Baseball Stadium Naming Rights

Team	Naming Rights	Sponsor	Total
New York Mets Citi Field (2006)	$400 million over 20 years; (opens in 2009)	Citigroup	$400 million
Houston Astros Minute Maid Park (2000)	$168 million over 28 years; $6 million average per year	The Coca–Cola Company	$168 million
Cincinnati Reds Great American Ball Park (2003)	$75 million over 30 years; $2.5 million average per year	Great American Insurance Group	$75 million
Chicago White Sox U.S. Cellular Field (1991)	$68 million over 23 years; $2.96 million average per year (expires 2026)		$68 million
Arizona Diamondbacks Bank One Ballpark (1998), now Chase Field (2005)	$66 million over 30 years; $2.2 million average per year (expires 2028)	Bank One Corporation, now Chase	$66 million
Detroit Tigers Comerica Park (2000)	$66 million over 30 years; $2.2 million average per year (expires 2030)	Comerica Bank	$66 million

Team/Stadium	Details	Sponsor	Amount
San Diego Padres Petco Park (2004)	$60 million over 22 years; $2.7 million average per year (expires 2026)	PETCO (the nation's #2 pet supply specialty retailer)	$60 million
Philadelphia Phillies Citizens Bank Park (2004)	$57.5 million over 25 years; $2.3 million average per year (expires 2029)	Citizens Bank	$57.5 million
Los Angeles Angels of Anaheim Edison International Field of Anaheim (1996)	$50 million over 20 years; $2.5 million average per year (expires 2018). Stadium name dropped after seven years; in 2003, it became the Angel Stadium of Anaheim.	Edison International	$50 million
San Francisco Giants Pacific Bell Park (2000)	$50 million over 24 years; $2.1 million average per year (expires 2024). The stadium is named AT&T Park as of 2006.	Pacific Bell	$50 million
Tampa Bay Rays Tropicana Field (1990)	$46 million over 30 years; $1.5 million average per year (expires 2026)	PepsiCo, Inc.	$46 million
Milwaukee Brewers Miller Park (2001)	$41 million over 20 years; $2.05 million average per year (expires 2020)	Miller Brewing Company	$41 million

(Continued)

EXHIBIT 1.5 (Continued)

Team	Naming Rights	Sponsor	Total
Seattle Mariners Safeco Field (1999)	$40 million over 20 years; $2 million average per year (expires 2019)	SafeCo	$40 million
Pittsburgh Pirates PNC Park (2001)	$30 million over 20 years; $1.5 million average per year (expires 2020)	PNC Financial Services	$30 million
Florida Marlins Pro Player Park/Stadium (1996–2006) Shared with Miami Dolphins football team	$20 million over 10 years; $2 million average per year (expired 2006). The stadium is now known as Dolphin Stadium; the Marlins must leave at the end of their current lease (2010). There's a new stadium being built for the team, who will be renamed the Miami Marlins.	Pro Player (sports apparel division of Fruit of the Loom)	$20 million

28

Team / Stadium	Contract	Named for	Amount
San Diego Padres QUALCOMM Stadium (1997) Shared with San Diego Chargers football team	$18 million over 20 years; $900,000 average per year (expires 2017). Padres relocated to Petco Park (see above) in 2004.	QUALCOMM Corporation	$18 million
Colorado Rockies Coors Field (1995)	$15 million; term of contract unavailable	Coors Brewing Company	$15 million
Cleveland Indians Jacobs Field (1994–2008)	$13.9 million over 20 years; $695,000 average per year (expires 2014). The stadium is named Progressive Field as of 2008.	Named for former team owners the Jacobs brothers	$13.9 million
Oakland Athletics Network Associates Coliseum (1998); now McAfee Stadium (2004) Shared with Oakland Raiders football team	$6 million over 5 years; $1.2 million per year. Original contract expired in 2003 and was renewed for a further 5 years and $6 million.	Network Associates, now McAfee	$12 million
Kansas City Royals Kauffman Stadium (1973)	None	Ownership family name	$1

Hot properties on the baseball stadium market include RFK Stadium, home of the Washington Nationals. Word on the street is that the ball club, formerly the Montreal Expos, will have a named stadium by the time they return in April 2008. On the west coast, the San Francisco Giants are reported to be in discussions with groups interested in renaming their baseball stadium.

Last but not least, the Detroit Tigers and Comerica Bank have had some talks about the continuation of the bank's name on the facility. Due to the hard times that have hit the Detroit area thanks to the downturn in the auto sector, Comerica has relocated its head office and much of its staff to Texas. Time will tell if this naming rights deal will stand as is.

Football Stadium Naming Rights

Football has long been one of America's favorite pastimes. With its unique scheduling, unlike any other pro sport, the National Football League (NFL) has legions of fans who follow their teams with passionate energy and focus. From the tailgate parties that may start the night before a weekly contest to the post-game interviews on television, the brand name of the stadium is front and center, entwining itself into the fabric of the event and the history of the game.

There are some things you just can't mess with, and sometimes, the name of a football stadium is one of them. In Denver, Colorado, when the naming rights to the stadium expired a few years ago and the new corporate label Invesco Field went up, the fans' protest was so dramatic that the corporate sponsor changed the name to satisfy them. The revised name incorporates a link with the past: Denver's and Colorado's football stadium is now called Invesco Field at Mile High Stadium.

Exhibit 1.6 shows the naming rights for the professional football sports leagues. There are 32 NFL teams, and only 18 of the stadiums have naming rights attached. Some of these teams' stadiums are unlikely to change names, including the Green Bay Packers' Lambeau Field in Green Bay, Wisconsin. The stadium took on that name in 1965 after the death of Curly Lambeau, a founder, player, and the first coach of the Green Bay Packers. First built in 1957, the stadium has had plenty of opportunities to add a new name during seven different upgrades—but some things are not for sale.

The revenue from naming rights deals may help some teams pay for the high-priced talent of free agents. On the other hand, teams that have pursued the free-agent market in an effort to improve the team have not always met with success; for example, consider the Washington Redskins.

The city of Jacksonville, Florida has proposed that it receive up to 25% of any naming rights agreement, in what would be one of the first municipality/pro football team revenue-sharing contracts. This is another precedent in the business.

Look for several headline stories from NFL football over the next two years, as new stadium deals are

EXHIBIT 1.6 National Football League Naming Rights

Stadium Name	Sponsor	Home Teams	Average Per Year	Expires
Alltel Stadium*	Alltel Corp.	Jacksonville Jaguars	$620,000	2007
Bank of America Stadium	Bank of America	Carolina Panthers	$7 million	2024
Edward Jones Dome	Edward Jones	St. Louis Rams	$2.65 million	2013
FedEx Field	Federal Express	Washington Redskins	$7.6 million	2025
Ford Field	Ford Motor Co.	Detroit Lions	$1 million	2042
Gillette Stadium	Gillette	New England Patriots	N/A	2017
Heinz Field	H.J. Heinz	Pittsburgh Steelers	$2.9 million	2021

* Alltel has declined to renew its option to continue as the naming rights sponsor of the football stadium as of summer 2007.

Invesco Field at Mile High	Invesco Funds	Denver Broncos	$6 million	2021
Lincoln Financial Field	Lincoln Financial Group	Philadelphia Eagles	$6.7 million	2022
LP Field	Louisiana–Pacific	Tennessee Titans	$3 million	2016
Lucas Oil Stadium	Lucas Oil	Indianapolis Colts	$6 million	2026
M & T Bank Stadium	M & T Bank	Baltimore Ravens	$5 million	2018
Monster Park	Monster Cable	San Francisco 49ers	$1.5 million	2007
Office Depot Center	Office Depot	Florida Panthers	$1.4 million	2013
Pro Player Stadium (now Dolphin Stadium)	Fruit of the Loom	Miami Dolphins, Florida Marlins	Company Bankrupt	2006

(Continued)

EXHIBIT 1.6 (Continued)

Stadium Name	Sponsor	Home Teams	Average Per Year	Expires
Qualcomm Stadium	Qualcomm	San Diego Chargers	$900,000	2017
Qwest Field	Qwest	Seattle Seahawks	$5 million	2019
Raymond James Stadium	Raymond James Financial	Tampa Bay Buccaneers	$3.1 million	2026
RCA Dome	RCA	Indianapolis Colts	$1 million	2004
Reliant Stadium	Reliant Energy	Houston Texans	$10 million	2032

announced. Will Texas become the top of the pile for pro football? What will happen with Oakland Coliseum or RFK Stadium?

Basketball Arena Naming Rights

Basketball enjoys the flexibility of being played in a multipurpose arena. In many cities, the NBA team shares a venue with a hockey team from the NHL and a women's basketball team from the WNBA. Event staff in these arenas often have to make the switch from a frozen ice surface for a hockey game to a basketball court overnight. Exhibit 1.7 shows the naming rights for the NBA. In the Home Teams column, you will see references to multiple teams that use the same facility, something that was not lost on the corporate sponsor.

Hockey Arena Naming Rights

In United States professional sports, hockey ranks a distant fourth behind baseball, football, and basketball—but it has an international following that the top three lack. In the early days of professional hockey, the Original Six teams straddled the American/Canadian border, with teams in Detroit, Toronto, Montreal, Chicago, New York, and Boston. It is interesting to note the international market for the game and, with that, the long-established cross-border sponsorship tradition.

As you review the list in Exhibit 1.8, take note of the home country of the naming sponsors of

EXHIBIT 1.7 National Basketball Association Naming Rights

Stadium Name	Sponsor	Home Teams	Average Per Year	Expires
American Airlines Arena	American Airlines	Miami Heat	$2.1 million	2019
American Airlines Center	American Airlines	Dallas Mavericks, Stars	$6.5 million	2031
America West Arena	America West	Phoenix Suns, Coyotes, Mercury	$866,667	2019
Arco Arena	Atlantic Richfield	Sacramento Kings, Monarchs	$750,000	2007
Barclays Arena	Barclays Bank	New Jersey Nets	$20 million	2028
Compaq Center	Compaq Computer	Houston Rockets, Comets	$900,000	2003
Conseco Fieldhouse	Conseco	Indiana Pacers, Fever	$2 million	2019
Continental Airlines Arena	Continental Airlines	New Jersey Nets	$1.4 million	2008

Delta Center	Delta Airlines	Utah Jazz, Starzz	$1.3 million	2011
FedEx Forum	Federal Express	Memphis Grizzlies	$4.5 million	2023
Wachovia Center	Wachovia Bank	Philadelphia 76ers, Flyers	$1.4 million	2023
Fleetcenter	Fleet Bank	Boston Celtics, Bruins	$2 million	2010
Gund Arena	Owners	Cleveland Cavs, Rockers	$700,000	2014
KeyArena	Key Corp.	Seattle Supersonics, Storm	$1 million	2010
MCI Center	MCI	Washington Wizards, Capitals, Mystics	$2.2 million	2017
Pepsi Center	PepsiCo	Denver Nuggets, Colorado Avalanche	$3.4 million	2019
Phillips Arena	Royal Phillips Electronics	Atlanta Hawks, Thrashers	$9.3 million	2019

(Continued)

EXHIBIT 1.7 (Continued)

Stadium Name	Sponsor	Home Teams	Average Per Year	Expires
SBC Center	SBC Communications	San Antonio Spurs	$2.1 million	2022
Staples Center	Staples	Los Angeles Lakers, Kings, Clippers, Sparks	$5.8 million	2019
Target Center	Target	Minnesota Timberwolves, Lynx	$1.3 million	2005
TD Waterhouse Centre	TD Waterhouse Group	Orlando Magic, Miracle	$1.6 million	2003
Toyota Center	Toyota	Houston Rockets	N/A	N/A
United Center	United Airlines	Chicago Bulls	$1.8 million	2014

EXHIBIT 1.8 National Hockey League Naming Rights

Arena	NHL Team	Naming Rights	Term	Expires	Total
Air Canada Centre	Toronto Maple Leafs	Air Canada	20	2019	$30 million
American Airlines Center	Dallas Stars	American Airlines	30	2031	$195 million
BankAtlantic Center	Florida Panthers	BankAtlantic	10	2015	$22 million
Bell Centre	Montreal Canadians	Bell Canada	20	2023	$64 million
Continental Airlines Arena	New Jersey Devils	Continental Airlines	12	2008	$29 million
Honda Center	Anaheim Bucks	Honda	15	2031	$60 million
General Motors Place	Vancouver Canucks	General Motors Canada	20	2015	$18.5 million
HP Pavilion at San Jose	San Jose Sharks	Hewlett–Packard	15	2016	$47 million

(Continued)

EXHIBIT 1.8 (Continued)

Arena	NHL Team	Naming Rights	Term	Expires	Total
HSBC Arena	Buffalo Sables	HSBC Bank	15	2016	$15 million
Jobing.com Arena	Phoenix Coyotes	Jobing.com	10	2016	$25 million
Mellon Arena	Pittsburgh Penguins	Mellon Financial	10	2009	$18 million
Nationwide Arena	Columbus Blue Jackets	Nationwide Insurance	Indefinite	None	See Below*
Pengrowth Saddledome	Calgary Flames	Pengrowth Management	20	2016	$20 million
Pepsi Center	Colorado Avalanche	Pepsi	20	2019	$68 million
Philips Arena	Atlanta Threshers	Philips Electronics	20	2019	$180 million
RBC Center	Carolina Hurricanes	RBC Centura Bank	20	2022	$80 million
Rexall Place	Edmonton Oilers	Rexall	10	2014	N/A

St. Pete Times Forum	Tampa Bay Lightening	St. Petersburg Times	12	2014	$25.2 million
Scotiabank Place	Ottawa Senators	Scotiabank	15	2021	$20 million
Scottrade Center**	St. Louis Blues	Scottrade Center	N/A	N/A	N/A
Sommet Center	Nashville Predators	Sommet Group	N/A	N/A	N/A
Staples Center	Los Angeles Kings	Staples	20	2019	$116 million
TD Banknorth Garden	Boston Bruins	TD Banknorth	20	2025	$120 million
United Center	Chicago Black Hawks	United Airlines	20	2014	$36 million
Verizon Center	Washington Capitals	Verizon	15	2017	$44 million
Wachovia Center	Philadelphia Flyers	Wachovia	29	2025	$40 million
Xcel Energy Center	Minnesota Wild	Xcel Energy	25	2024	$75 million

*Nationwide received naming rights indefinitely as part of a deal to provide 90% of the financing for the Columbus arena.
**Details of Scottrade's deal with St. Louis were not available, but it is believed to be in the range of $2 million to $4 million per year.

these arenas. For now, the international ownership of naming rights is much more prevalent in the game of professional hockey than it is baseball.

The second item to note is the dispersion of the corporate industries represented on the list. We find airlines, banks, telecommunications firms, automobile makers, computer and technology companies, newspapers, dot-com businesses, energy companies, and office supply companies. Quite a mix, isn't it? More than 40% of the hockey arenas that are home to an NHL team are named for a consumer product or services company. This is followed by naming rights owned by financial services companies and airlines.

The impact of brand name recognition is the primary motivation for a company acquiring naming rights. With hockey teams being just one of the tenants in the building, the companies that bought the naming rights are enjoying additional marketing exposure thanks to the other events such as concerts, trade shows. Multipurpose venues appear to be a popular choice and we can expect to see this trend continue and expand down to include smaller multipurpose facilities in smaller markets.

Only three teams play in stadiums without corporate naming rights attached to them: the Detroit Red Wings, in Joe Louis Arena; the New York Rangers, in Madison Square Garden; and the New York Islanders, in Nassau County Coliseum. The first two are unlikely to change, but the New York Islanders are the most likely NHL team to have naming rights come available sometime soon.

In late September 2007, Bill Wirtz, the owner of the Chicago Black Hawks, passed away. Wirtz had been instrumental in working with Chicago Bulls ownership to land the naming rights deal for the United Center, but he refused to allow the broadcast of hockey games on local TV. Brand name and brand value have a direct correlation with visibility in the market. Maybe that will change in Chicago.

Golf Tournament Sponsorships

The Professional Golfers Association (PGA) Tour features the most recognizable name in pro sports, Tiger Woods. That fact alone has had a lightning-rod effect on tournament sponsorships. Television ratings, the standard measure of viewership statistics, have bolted upwards for PGA events over the last two years, a fact not lost on corporate America.

One such example is the Northern Trust Open, played in California in February 2008. Northern Trust is a leading wealth management company that hopes to boost awareness of its brand in major markets with a recently announced five-year naming rights deal to sponsor this annual PGA Tour event. Although Northern Trust is far from a household name, a weekend of prime-time viewing on television, helped along by proverbial underdog Phil Mickelson winning his 33rd PGA tour event at the Northern Trust Open, brought the brand to the consumers' consciousness.

The British are Coming!
The British are Coming!

What say you, scout? The British are coming to America?

It's true. And there's no need for the lanterns in Paul Revere fashion; the Brits are already here.

The NBA's New Jersey Nets recently had $400 million worth of British money land in their pockets from global banking giant Barclays Bank of London, UK. The Nets' new facility will be called Barclays Arena—the first time a British company has ventured into the United States. Barclays snapped up one of the juiciest sports properties on the market. The announcement in May 2007 came less than eight months after rival Citigroup signed a similar naming deal for $400 million with the cross-town New York Mets of major league baseball.

At first glance, New Yorkers might think that Citigroup is the clear winner in this one. People know the Citigroup brand name as one of America's leading financial services providers. According to an annual survey published by Interbrand, a company that puts a ranking number on the value of brand names, the Citi brand sits at number 11 on the Best Global Brands list, behind Coca Cola, Microsoft, and IBM (www.businessweek.com/pdfs/2007/0732_globalbrands.pdf). Further, Citigroup has a significant presence in the greater New York area and an established client base. The naming rights deal is one more way to deepen the relationships with existing customers and attract new ones.

When the first pitch is thrown out in 2009, Citi Field will be home to 81 ball games. That's half of the 162-game schedule, and perhaps more if the team makes it into the playoffs.

Along comes Barclays. On the global stage of financial services, Barclays Bank (www.barclays.co .uk) is the heavyweight, and Citigroup the underling. The British firm has a long-standing relationship with the New York financial community, including brokerage houses, the New York Stock Exchange, and member institutions. But if you read through the full list of the Best Global Brands, you won't find Barclays anywhere on that list.

At the time of the announcement, Barclays Bank did not even have a single retail banking location in New York City. In January 2007, Barclays paid $225 million to acquire EquiFirst, the 12th-largest subprime whole mortgage originator in the United States, with 600 employees in Charlotte, North Carolina. EquiFirst works with more than 9,000 mortgage brokers in 47 states and will be merged into the Barclays Capital division of the multinational corporation.

Barclays is no stranger to sports properties. The bank is the title sponsor of the Barclays Premier League Web site for English football, which features daily updates about team and players (www. premierleague.com/page/Home/0,,12306,00.html). Barclays regards sports properties as extensions of its global marketing plan. Gaining a share of the wallet in New York, as they like to say in financial circles, is high on the British bank's agenda.

The scenario is reminiscent of what Key Bank pulled off in Seattle 20 years ago when they bought the naming rights to the venue that plays host to the NBA's Seattle Supersonics. At the time, Key Bank had just made a series of retail banking acquisitions in the Seattle area and was looking for something to give its marketing a shot in the arm. Since its acquisition of the naming rights to the Supersonics' arena, Key Bank has grown into a market leader with tremendous brand name presence in the local community. If you happen to do a Google search of the name, you will find that the Key Bank Arena is not just a basketball floor for the NBA, but a year-round entertainment facility that includes concerts, sports, trade shows, and other high-profile events.

In recent years, Japanese car makers Toyota and Honda bought the naming rights to multi-event arenas in the western part of the United States. The Toyota Center in Houston features the NBA's Houston Rockets as its main tenant, and the Honda Center in Anaheim bills itself as southern California's premier sports and entertainment center. It is no coincidence that Japanese cars are selling well in these regions and are on track to continue to gain market share.

Honda certainly got plenty of mileage during the 2006–2007 NHL season, as the resident Anaheim Ducks made it to the finals and won the Stanley Cup, representing hockey supremacy. Media coverage is the marketing department's nirvana, especially television broadcasts from the Honda Center—it just doesn't get any better than that. Over and over again during those events, the media referenced the named facility. This sort of presence in the marketplace is exactly what naming rights acquisition is all about.

HSBC, the world's largest bank, acquired the naming rights to the Buffalo Sabres' hockey arena, now called the HSBC Arena. In this case, an international corporation came to the United States, land of opportunity as the old saying goes, to steal away the naming rights for a paltry $800,000 a year because there were few others interested in the deal to bid up the price at the time. What a good call that was, compared to the going rate to get a named venue with television coverage and multipurpose functionality.

Two years ago, the Royal Bank of Canada, another foreign entity that bought a named venue in the United States, celebrated with gusto as their own feature tenant, the Carolina Hurricanes of the NHL, won the title.

In a September 18, 2007 press release, the Royal Bank of Canada noted that it was getting good value for the $4 million a year it is paying to name the RBC Center in Raleigh, North Carolina. The multipurpose arena plays host not only to the NHL's Carolina Hurricanes but also to the North Carolina State University basketball team—talk about a one-two punch! The basketball team alone brought the bank enormous exposure and brand-building for the RBC Centura name after the parent company began a series of retail bank acquisitions about four years ago in the southeast United States.

A recent study by a sports marketing firm in the area points to positive feedback in terms of media hits and feedback from locals who go to the arena. The Canadian bank has an $80 million commitment to the region that extends more than a decade. This is another example of a long-term marketing plan rolling out as it should.

Some might say, "Big deal, it's just hockey." It's true that hockey is not as popular as football and baseball, but the real value to the owners of a named sports venue, especially one that is a multipurpose facility, is the amount of media coverage that comes from being in the sponsorship game.

Citi Field will be home to 81 New York Mets baseball games starting in 2009. The Barclays Arena will be a state-of-the-art multipurpose facility positioned to challenge the venerable Madison Square Garden for top-flight entertainment dates.

The 20-year naming rights deal is already starting to pay dividends for both companies. In the international realm of wealth management, clients use international tax treaties, foreign investments, and 24/7 stock markets around the world to manage their wealth. New York, the Big Apple, is home to a lot of money. Barclays has just taken its first bite of that apple.

The British are coming! The British are coming!

~ 2 ~

Naming Traditions,
Then and Now

Naming traditions have been around for hundreds of years. The tradition of granting naming rights in exchange for money has been gaining momentum over the last three decades. The escalating sticker prices for high-profile, scarce properties have fundraising executives rethinking their short- and long-term strategies and, with that, making radical changes to the status quo. In this chapter, we will explore naming rights traditions, then and now.

Recently, the trend has been toward a greater selection of naming rights from organizations large and small. Like a residential homeowner eyeing a red-hot seller's market, an ever-increasing number of nonprofits are listing their inventory of naming opportunities to major gift prospects. Since the mid-1990s, there has been a groundswell of naming rights activity. Not only nonprofits but other organizations as well, including municipalities, state and federal government departments, are out there marketing their shopping list to would-be supporters. My own research suggests that 2007 was a banner year for naming rights deals in this sector. American nonprofits are estimated to have logged over $4 billion, including named endowments, over the last 12-month period. In Canada, the estimate tops the $300 million mark. Not so sure about those numbers? Check out the chart below:

List of Top 12 Named Gifts to Nonprofits in the USA—2007

Sanford Health System Sioux City, SD	$400 million
Robert Day Scholars Program Claremont McKenna College, CA	$200 million
Kosair Children's Hospital, KY	$130 million
University of California, Berkeley Hewlett Packard Foundation Grant for 100 Endowed Professorships	$113 million
University of Washington Gates Institute for Health Metrics and Evaluation	$105 million
Moorehead Foundation Scholarship gift University of North Carolina	$100 million
McNair Campus, Houston Baylor College of Medicine	$100 million

Lurie Chidrens' Memorial Hospital, Chicago	$100 million
Oregon Athletics Legacy Fund University of Oregon	$100 million
Betty Irene Moore School of Nursing University of California, Davis	$100 million
University of Illinois in Urbana, Champaign Gift from Tom Siebel to academic endowments	$100 million
Warren Alpert Medical School Brown University, RI	$100 million

Those 12 named gifts add up to $1.64 billion in naming rights. Over and above these naming gifts are three other gifts of $100 million made in 2007 from anonymous donors. Their generosity is felt by many, their names known to but a few. Choosing not to be publicly recognized in typical naming tradition is a matter of personal privacy, something that is done more frequently these days.

The next 16 named gifts made in 2007 add up to another $595 million. Combined they add up to more than $2 billion in named gifts from 28 donors. Based on the data shown above and on my research work, *The National Survey of Naming Opportunities and Named Gifts*, I estimate that the nonprofit sector had approximately $4 billion in named gifts announced in 2007—an unofficial record.

BIG ROCKS TOSSED
INTO A SMALL POND

We all know what happens when we toss big rocks into a small pond, don't we? There is an immediate splash relative to the size of the rock and the size of the pond. The ripple effect extends outward in all directions. I maintain that this not unlike the effect of what happens when major gifts come in during a fundraising effort.

When we consider the number of billion-dollar campaigns currently underway, more than 50 and counting, along with their respective campaign goals, I predict that 2008 will be another record-setting year for named gifts, topping the $5 billion mark in total.

How did this corner of the nonprofit sector become so dynamic, so vibrant? What does it say about the times we live in when the fundraising campaigns of a local university or hospital transcend the needs of the institution itself and become focal points of economic development?

THEORY OF THE CAPITAL
CAMPAIGN MULTIPLIER EFFECT

Fundraising is no longer only about the financial legacy of the campaign for the organization. Large fundraising campaigns and the naming rights gifts they attract bring waves of new jobs, starting with new staff to run the campaign right through to completion of the construction several years hence.

The movement of large amounts of money through a community is referred to as economic development. It is typically measured by a technique referred to as the multiplier effect. Politicians and civil servants talk about the multiplier effect of a trade show or international conference that brings tourists to town, or that of a new employer moving into the city, town, or region, bringing new jobs.

I maintain that the fundraising campaigns going on across the country leave a deeper imprint in the economic landscape than the arrival and departure of the annual flow of tourists and convention attendees. And because of their long-term effects they should be given more credit in the overall economic matrix.

For every dollar raised in the campaign, there is a multiplier effect that spirals through the organization and out into the community. The payroll of the organization may increase or achieve a new level of financial certainty prior to the naming rights gift(s). In turn, the staff spends their paychecks on housing, cars, groceries, and other living expenses, and the money flows through the local economy.

The impact of multimillion dollar naming gifts crosses the boundary of one individual leaving a legacy for the recipient organization. It helps us all.

So how did we get here? I think we can find some answers when we look back and examine the melding together of naming traditions with necessity.

"NAMED IN HONOR OF..."
—A TRADITION FADING FAST

As you look around your own community, you will no doubt be able to find plenty of examples of a building or place that was named in honor of someone. A bird's-eye view of North America reveals thousands of cities, towns, rivers, lakes, and roads named for someone or someplace across the Atlantic. Settlers who came to the New World brought with them memories of the places and people they respected and revered. The label given to the city of "New" York and "New" Jersey have historic links back to the city of York and the island of Jersey in England.

In the state of Massachusetts alone, we find Bedford, Brockton, Cambridge, Chatham, and Gloucester, all named after towns in England. In Canada, the English influence is even more significant, as the northern country had a longer living arrangement with the Brits than did their U.S. cousins.

In New Paltz, New York, people there say that The Street of the Huguenots is the oldest named street in the country. The Huguenots originally came from France, part of a Protestant religious group that immigrated to the New World. Historical records show the first landing of Huguenots on May 1, 1562 at St. John's River in Florida, according to the National Huguenot Society. In 1585, the Huguenots were expelled from France and began an outward migration looking for new homes. 100 years later, religious persecution led to a mass exodus of 400,000 Huguenots and Protestants to countries around the world. They went looking for a country where they would be safe and allowed to practice their religious beliefs. Those who settled in the United States named streets to honor their ancestors, like the one in New Paltz.

Naming traditions were born out of the events and lives of people like the Huguenots. They helped to set the bar for what would follow. In the education field, we can point to several keys naming events that helped to establish benchmarks for the first colleges and universities.

In Williamsburg, Virginia, the College of William and Mary, the second oldest university in the United States, was chartered in 1693 by King William III and Queen Mary II of England and bears the names of both English monarchs. Naming a university in the American colonies after British royalty was considered a high tribute to the distant king and queen.

The Marshall-Wythe School of Law at the College of William and Mary was so designated in 1953, followed the institution's naming tradition. The joint name is a tribute to John Marshall, an alumnus who went on to become one of the first Justices of the Supreme Court of the United States, and George Wythe, the first holder of the Chair of Law created in 1779 at the College of William and Mary. Wythe was instrumental in developing the course curriculum for the school of law, along with other notable achievements, including his roles as a leader in the struggle for independence, a signer of the Declaration of Independence, and a leader in American legal education.

Visitors to Washington, D.C. can find many named spaces and places throughout the nation's capital. The statue at the Lincoln Memorial is named for President Abraham Lincoln, nearby Arlington House is a tribute to General Robert E. Lee, and the Franklin Delano Roosevelt Memorial honors the former President. Each one is a national monument with historic significance, named to honor the memory of American leaders.

We can see how these naming traditions created by the federal government set the pattern for naming traditions at the state and local level. Naming initiatives like these helped to set the framework, or guidelines as some would call them, for what it meant to have a place or property named for someone. But this tradition is fading fast from the American landscape. School boards, municipalities, and government agencies are joining thousands of nonprofit organizations on the "let's sell the naming rights!" bandwagon.

THREE TYPES OF NAMING RIGHTS

As you move through the content of this book, keep in mind the three distinct types of naming rights traditions that exist today:

1. Naming rights for a legacy gift
2. Naming rights for a title sponsor of an event
3. Naming rights for a long-term corporate partner

The government was not alone in creating the naming rights tradition. Along the way, people were helping create the identity of independent states and regions in the formative years of the nation. Part of that identity was defined by philanthropists, wealthy people who stepped up and decided they wanted to make a difference without government involvement.

Naming Rights for a Legacy Gift

Naming rights granted in exchange for a legacy gift became more common in the 1900s. As prosperity levels rose in the late 1890s and into the start of the next century, an upper class of financially well-off individuals and families emerged. Their wealth came from industry and commerce, such as banking, forestry, mining, oil, and gas, and manufacturing. One at a time, they began to get involved in offering financial support to a wide range of charitable initiatives.

The Rockefeller family, for example, is legendary for their generosity and philanthropic support. People like the Rockefellers helped to create new opportunities for education, arts, and culture groups; to build libraries; and to lay the foundation for accomplishment that we enjoy today.

The Rockefeller Center in midtown Manhattan is named after billionaire John D. Rockefeller, the founder of Standard Oil and one of the wealthiest men in America at the time. He had leased 11 acres of land from Columbia University in 1928 and planned to revitalize the area with the construction of the Metropolitan Opera House and office buildings. The stock market crash of 1929 forced him to change his plans, and instead he decided to develop an art deco–style collection of 19 office buildings instead.

The Rockefeller Institute for Medical Research in New York, was founded in 1901 by John D. Rockefeller and later renamed The Rockefeller University. The Rockefeller College of Public Affairs & Policy at the State University of New York, Albany was named after him. And the John D. Rockefeller, Jr. Library at Colonial Williamsburg was named for him as well.

John D. Rockefeller did not confine his philanthropy to the United States. Numerous facilities around the world are named for his charitable support, including the Rockefeller Archaeological Museum in Jerusalem and the Rockefeller Music Hall in Oslo, Norway.

In 2005, his grandson, David Rockefeller, Jr., donated $100 million to New York's Museum of Modern Art endowment fund. The museum itself was co-founded by David's mother, Abby. Reports from the Museum of Modern Art indicate that the 89-year-old philanthropist had contributed in excess of $200 million to the museum up to that year.

Abby got involved in another museum project in Colonial Williamsburg. Her contribution was so significant that the facility is named in her honor: the Abby Aldrich Rockefeller Folk Art Museum.

Other famous Americans who have been recognized with naming rights include Caroline Wiess Law, who left a $300 million bequest to the Houston Museum of Fine Arts. Her gift is on record as the largest cash contribution ever given a museum in the country.

Contemporary philanthropist Joan Kroc, widow of McDonald's founder Ray Kroc, gave away $2.3 billion during her life, often without the fanfare of the naming rights conferred on others. At her death, among other gifts, she left $200 million to National Public Radio and $50 million to the University of Notre Dame to strengthen the Joan B. Kroc Institute for International Peace Studies, after previous gifts of $6 million to establish the Institute and $14 million in general support. These are some of the many gifts from the woman who liked to be known as a maverick philanthropist. At one point Kroc set up a foundation, as was the custom at the time, and began to take applications. She shut it down, citing too much paperwork. The legend of Joan Kroc suggests that if you asked for money it would not come. She was a free spirit who chose to follow her intuition and spontaneous assessment of the moment. Joan Kroc was one of the most generous and intriguing philanthropists of all time.

CHANGING TRADITIONS

The changing traditions regarding naming rights are not only about how big the sign is on the outside of the building and what kind of material is being used. In Exhibit 2.1, you will find a side-by-side comparison chart that highlights the many activities that go into securing a naming rights legacy gift.

The higher education sector provides numerous examples of naming rights conferred on a donor in appreciation of their legacy gift. Hastings College of the Law at the University of California was founded by Serranus Clinton Hastings, who was the first Chief Justice of the California Supreme Court. In 1878, he paid $100,000 into the State Treasury for the establishment of California's first public law school.

Given the naming rights tradition at the time, it seemed most appropriate to name the college after Hastings, a tradition that lives on today. Exhibit 2.1 offers a side-by-side comparison of many of the aspects that impact the naming rights process both then and now. For illustrative purposes, I have chosen to use the example of Hastings College of the Law to compare the naming traditions of 1878 to their modern-day versions.

Comparing naming traditions then and now is an interesting exercise, if only to see how the sector has evolved. Since the 1800s, the fundraising office has added layers of infrastructure, including staff members dedicated to donor relations and, more recently, an office of stewardship to go along

EXHIBIT 2.1 Hastings College of the Law

Naming Traditions in the Past Assume the Year 1878 and the Legacy Gift to Name Hastings College of the Law at University of California	Naming Traditions Today Name a Prominent School or College
Prospect Identification: Small circle of people In many cases, the donor stepped up and volunteered to make a gift without being asked. Planned gifts came from occasional bequests.	**Prospect Identification:** Global search potential Examples of unexpected named gifts continue. The formal structure of Planned Giving programs resonates with the Baby Boomer generation, resulting in the receipt of an increasing number of major gifts named posthumously for the donor.
Make the Ask: Ask made by a known peer of the prospect, or gift volunteered by the individual.	**Make the Ask:** Ask made by volunteer and development staff.
Naming Gift Price Range: $500 to $100,000	**Naming Gift Price Range:** $25,000 to $500 million+

(Continued)

61

EXHIBIT 2.1 (Continued)

Naming Traditions in the Past Assume the Year 1878 and the Legacy Gift to Name Hastings College of the Law at University of California	Naming Traditions Today Name a Prominent School or College
Naming Gift Ask Amounts: There were a lot fewer naming opportunities available; hence, the ask amounts were within a much narrower dollar range than today. 130 years ago, when Hastings College of the Law was named, the relative value of $100,000 was worth substantially more than it is today.	**Naming Gift Ask Amounts:** $100 to $100 million+ The most noticeable difference today is the market segmention of elite level groups and how much they ask for a naming gift compared to small-to medium-sized nonprofits. For example, the ask amount to name a business school greatly depends on which, university is being referring to. A divison-three university may only be able to ask for $8 million to $12 million to name its business school, compared to a Top 50 university for which the ask amount could range from $25 million to $50 million.

Naming Rights Policy Statement: Not in use	**Naming Rights Policy Statement:** Common practice in more than 75% of universities and colleges. How often the policy statements are updated to reflect current views is another topic.
Naming Ceremony: The cutting of the Red Ribbon was included, with many naming ceremonies, with stakeholders, family, and traditional media in attendance.	**Naming Ceremony:** The cutting of the Red Ribbon is included in the high-profile named gift, with stakeholders in attendance. Traditional media may or may not attend. There may be an unveiling of naming recognition on the building, the donor walls, or a new organization logo for gifts where dollar amount is significant.
Signage: Suitable outdoor signage was used, with little thought given to the impact of brand name.	**Signage:** Suitable outdoor signage can be extended to the letterhead of the organization and all organizational media material to extend and boost the value of the brand name, such as the Web site, newsletters, annual report, and other communications. The value of virtual signage is growing rapidly.

(Continued)

EXHIBIT 2.1 (Continued)

Naming Traditions in the Past Assume the Year 1878 and the Legacy Gift to Name Hastings College of the Law at University of California	Naming Traditions Today Name a Prominent School or College
Donor Involvement after Making the Naming Gift: Low level of involvement by donor, often times none at all, as donors had a very high level of trust in the people in charge of charitable organizations.	**Donor Involvement after Making the Naming Gift:** Tends to be more involved, with higher expectations of accountability and disclosure. Some named gift donors are very involved after the gift has been made.
Stewardship: Not considered to be a high priority with most nonprofits. Stewardship activities are found mainly in local and regional church parishes and cathedrals regarding the distribution of funds for overseas missionary work.	**Stewardship:** Ongoing, attend to living donors by dedicated donor relations staff. Recent trends show a dramatic increase in the importance of stewardship activities and long-term relationships with donors. There is a greater emphasis today on donor retention than in 1878.

Media coverage:
Newspaper article

Which Organization to Receive the Naming Gift:
Universities and colleges got the majority of major gifts that wound up being named for the donor. This included gifts to name the schools of business, law, and engineering.

Current traditions of major gift donors include applying the policy and tactics of moves management to encourage subsequent major gifts.

Media coverage:
Newspaper, radio, online video, Web site news article, Web site, historical notes, and Annual Report to Donors

Which Organization to Receive the Naming Gift:
Trends suggest that donors are spreading their wealth around to other nonprofits outside the higher education sector.

Competition for the high-dollar-value naming rights gifts are being challenged by nonprofits in health care, social services, environmental, youth organizations, and other groups outside the nonprofit sector, including cities, state, and federal government agencies.

with the annual giving and planned giving departments. The other significant change is the development of and consistent application of naming policies for an organization.

A challenge for contemporary fundraising executives appears to be making time to review and update those naming policies and the accompanying ask amounts for naming opportunities. Most development staff appear to wait until the start of a campaign to think about updating the naming policies. Determining which properties are going to be included in the list of available naming opportunities is something that should be done sooner rather than later in the planning process. For more on that subject, see Chapter 6, "Manager's Toolbox for Naming Rights."

As we reflect on the history of naming rights, we see other examples of people volunteering to give without being asked. A number of these can be found among the western settlers, whose pioneer spirit embraced many possibilities as they helped to build America.

One day a few years ago I happened to witness one such event. I can recall the look of surprise and delight of a scholarship officer walking through the development office, sharing the news of a $73,000 check that had just arrived. It was accompanied by a brief handwritten note from a prospect turned donor, whom he had met with the week before. The university in turn set up a named scholarship endowment for the donor.

You may have heard it said that the best ask is the one that is not made. Meeting with and talking to the donors about the mission and vision of the campaign has led to many a major gift.

A SIGN OF THE TIMES

Another tradition that has carried forward to modern days is the ceremony involved in changing the name of the property. In the old days, new signage was created and attached, engraved, or added to the structure, followed shortly afterward by a ribbon-cutting ceremony to officially open the area to the public. The tradition in the 1800s of the transfer of naming rights included a public ceremony, ribbon cutting, and an article in the local newspaper.

Today, naming gift ceremonies are taking on a much more vibrant style as multimedia outlets get involved in the event. There is so much competition for people's attention these days. Many nonprofits enlist the help of dedicated marketing and communications staff to get the message out. Tactics and strategies include the tried-and-true approach of gathering a collection of stakeholders at the naming event, digital broadcast of the event, and electronic messaging.

Nonprofits have found they can effectively leverage technology to spread the word and share the moment with their donor community via e-mail announcements and Web site broadcasts that can be archived for viewing again. A few groups have gone so far as to include an audio recording of the naming ceremony on their Web sites, something I think we will see more of in the future.

TODAY'S WEALTHY AMERICANS AND NAMED PROPERTIES

For many of the richest people in America, like Bill and Melinda Gates, Warren Buffet, Oprah Winfrey, Tiger Woods, and Lance Armstrong, a named gift to a nonprofit organization is something that is done sparingly. Don't get me wrong. These people are incredibly generous in their financial support. It's just that the list of facilities or properties that have their names on them are few. Many appear to take this route because they do not want to take away from the work being done by the recipient organization; others choose to intentionally stay out of the spotlight, as Joan Kroc did. Often, they prefer to step back from the limelight and make a "quiet contribution" to a favorite charity. The lack of name recognition does not diminish the thanks and appreciation from those who received the financial support.

The nonprofit sector itself is full of wonderful examples of philanthropic gifts that have been honored with naming rights. In the majority of cases, they are named in perpetuity. Naming in perpetuity is something else that is quickly changing.

Naming Rights for a Long-Term Corporate Partner

The corporate sector appears to be increasing its focus on naming rights within the nonprofit sector on several fronts. The corporation's marketing and sponsorship staff seek to align the corporation's interest with events, programs, institutes, and facilities that fit the demographic mix of their customers. Corporations are attempting to get the most bang for their marketing buck, we all know that. It's an important distinction to keep in mind when having a conversation with a prospective corporate donor or sponsor as compared to a conversation with an individual or private foundation who might wish to give a purely philanthropic gift.

In recent years, many of our public traditions have been absorbed by corporations seeking naming rights to enhance recognition of their brand names. Why? To take advantage of the acute focus that the general public brings to holidays, special events, and other happenings.

But did the corporate sector take a page from the nonprofit sector when it came to acquiring naming rights? In the United States and Canada, there is a long-standing tradition of philanthropic support. Choosing to have a philanthropic perspective is a tradition that has been passed along in many families. Name recognition for designated support is another tradition that began hundreds of years ago. It is one that has gained momentum in recent times.

New Year's Eve, for example, brings with it a multitude of corporate naming initiatives in the annual celebrations. It's the biggest party that just keeps getting bigger, as the global population pushes past the 6 billion mark. From Tokyo to Times Square to Sydney to Paris, corporations have been buying up the advertising and naming rights to events far and wide. In turn, we have been treated with a televised spectacle complete with fireworks, symphony orchestras, and dare I say it, a beloved tradition of counting down those last few seconds. 10, 9, 8, as hundreds of millions join in to ring in the New Year, 7, 6, 5, champagne glasses raised in salute, 4, 3, 2, 1, hugs and kisses and well wishes all around. Happy New Year!

How do you bring in the New Year? If you are within a certain age demographic, you can be certain that the marketing staff and advertising agencies are working on ways to attract your eyeballs to their promotional material. New Year's Eve celebrations are a high-profile place to be seen. For the marketers, it's not about direct sales—it's more along the line of product and brand name recognition.

New Year's Eve celebrations are a good starting point to examine corporate naming rights at traditional events. Think about how the corporate sector gets involved in your community. Look at the pre-event marketing material, and the materials used the evening of the event.

Many a nonprofit organization has unique events and get-togethers, each one wrapped in its own traditions. For example, opening night at the North

American Auto Show, which is held annually in downtown Detroit, Michigan. The tradition includes a Charity Preview event. On January 18, 2008, the Charity Preview was held—a black tie affair that cost was $400 per ticket to attend. The funds raised from ticket sales this year went to Detroit youth groups such as the local Boys and Girls Clubs, Easter Seals—Michigan, Detroit Children's Hospital, March of Dimes, the Judson Center, and Think Detroit PAL.

The Charity Preview in Detroit, like many other events, is typically supported not only by ticket sales but also by corporate sponsors who pay for naming rights to be associated with the event. January 2008 saw the Royal Bank of Scotland Group, Charter One, and Sprint all getting involved in this international event, which garners television, print media and on-site promotional opportunities.

What I find most interesting in the growing trend of corporations buying naming rights from nonprofit groups is the scope of these actions and the accompanying dollar values involved. Here are some incidents of naming rights being bought up at high schools:

- November 23, 2007—In Hueber Heights, Ohio, Good Samaritan Hospital acquired the naming rights and marketing strategies for Wayne High School athletics. The hospital has a new health center under construction and has committed to investing $1.5 million over 10 years in exchange for the naming rights.

- March 20, 2007—An Indiana school board cut a deal to sell naming rights. Forum Credit Union agreed to pay $26,000 over the next three years to refurbish the Hall of Champions wing in Fishers High School. It marked the first time this school board had sold naming rights to a sponsor.
- 2006—Prior to the naming agreement at Fishers High School, another Indiana school completed a more substantial deal. Officials from Noblesville High School accepted $125,000 from Hare Chevrolet in exchange for the naming rights to the high school football field.
- June 20, 2006—Acuity Insurance of Wisconsin secured the naming rights to the Plymouth High School Auditorium in Sheboygan, Wisconsin, for $300,000. This was Acuity's second major gift to a high school in the community that year; in January 2006, Acuity made a gift of $650,000 for naming rights to the new North and South High School field houses in the Sheboygan Area School District.

Corporate support in the form of named sponsorships has been around for decades. A visit to just about any university or college Web site will offer a list of current named sponsors for the institution. The interesting part is that some of these corporate partners are spreading their wings and "investing in" other named properties. Take a look at the following list to see what I mean.

January 19, 2008

PACCAR Hall named University of Washington, Seattle	$18 million
January 18, 2008	
Harris Corp. Institute for Assured Information	
Florida Institute of Technology, Orlando	$5 million
January 16, 2008	
Bank of America Ctr. for Banking & Financial Studies	
Florida State University	$2 million

Corporate philanthropy is nothing new. What appears to be changing is the style and manner of corporate support. There appears to be a growing trend for corporations to ask for and get public naming rights in exchange for the dollars they are investing in nonprofit organizations.

More evidence of this emerging trend is the $25 million naming rights acquisition by AT&T. The company now has naming rights to the AT&T Executive Education and Conference Center at the University of Texas, Arlington. It's a 25-year limited term naming rights deal that resembles a private sector naming arrangement for an athletic venue such as a ball park or football stadium. It gives AT&T a strategic location that provides high-profile brand name recognition for the telecom giant, which has been facing increasing competition in the state of Texas.

Those of you who follow college football are well aware of how corporate naming rights to bowl games have expanded over the years (partial list below).

- PapaJohns.com Bowl
- Insight Bowl
- Meineke Car Care Bowl
- MPC Computers Bowl
- GMAC Bowl
- Chick-fil-A Bowl
- Capital One Bowl

Allow me to touch on one more aspect of corporate naming rights as we wrap up this chapter, something that I think we will see sooner rather than later: a corporate name appearing on a prominent school or college at a major university. Is it too much of a stretch to consider the Kodak School of Performing Arts or the TRW School of Engineering? Both are hypothetical examples and not meant as projected happenings. However, I don't think corporate naming rights for schools and colleges is a matter of *if* it will happen, but *when*.

~ 3 ~

Impact of the Internet on Naming Rights

> ...when I talk to our donors about our campaign, the next thing they do is to go to our Web site....

This is the type of comment I have heard over and over during the past two years from senior development staff. It's easy to understand why.

According to Internet World Stats (www.inter networldstats.com/emarketing.htm), the number of Internet users has grown from 16 million in 1995 to more than 1.32 billion as of December 2007. Annual growth is in excess of 17%.

LEVELING THE PLAYING FIELD

The Internet has helped to level the playing field for small businesses relative to the corporate giants. One Web site is just as accessible as another. And the same can be said about the nonprofit sector. As of 2006, there were more than 1,478,154 registered non-profit organizations in the United States, according to the National Center for Charitable Statistics. Hundreds of thousands of them have Web sites.

A Web site is vital in the competitive world of major gift giving. As a prospective donor enters the URL that leads to a Web site, they are just key strokes away from making that connection. Those few precious seconds when someone chooses to access one Web site address rather than another is part of the level playing field. In the electronic domain of the Internet, all have equal access, all have equal presence, and all are equally accessible.

For the smaller nonprofit organizations this equal access/equal presence is a double-edged sword. On one hand, the Internet allows them to create and deliver Web sites that reach out to prospective donors just like the most successful universities and colleges, hospitals, social service agencies, and other nonprofits that raise the majority of fundraising dollars each year. On the other hand, those Web sites should be maintained with regular updates, which can be difficult to do when time and resources are in short supply.

When it comes to online naming rights, the concept of the level playing field is a natural extension of the Web site. From promoting special events to capital campaigns, the Web site has become an ideal marketing tool to quickly update and inform the donor community about what's going on. Opportunities to promote naming properties are growing exponentially.

Take named endowments as an example. In the higher education sector, where universities hold vast sums of money in named endowment accounts, survey results suggest that an increasing number of donors are choosing to receive their endowment reports electronically instead of the traditional hard-copy version.

INTERNET TRENDS FOR NONPROFIT WEB SITES

Listed below are some of the most prominent Internet trends relating to nonprofit Web sites. When we look at these trends as a whole, we can see the depth and magnitude of the impact that the Internet has had on the nonprofit sector.

- Nonprofit Web sites are evolving.
- Online giving continues to boom.
- Online planned giving appears to be maturing.
- Electronic marketing by e-mail and online newsletters has increased.
- Naming rights for high-profile named gifts include the acquisition of Web site named properties.
- The format and style of donor recognition to naming rights is becoming standardized on Web sites.
- Fundraising campaigns are carried out within dedicated sections of nonprofits' Web sites.

Advanced Donor Relations Strategy

The final item in the above list, fundraising campaigns with dedicated pages on the Web site, is a splendid example of what I refer to as advanced donor relations. Campaign Web sites have risen to a new level in recent years. They have evolved in style and content, taking on greater significance.

One element of advanced donor relations related to nonprofit Web sites is the ease-of-use quotient, which measures how quickly and easily a Web site visitor can find what they are looking for on the Web site. Web site navigation starts at the home page. Studies show that in the time it takes to blink twice, a Web site visitor has already formed an opinion of how comfortable he or she is in navigating a Web site. The implication for online naming rights and naming rights recognition of sponsors and legacy gift donors is critically important.

When a donor is being recognized for making a naming rights gift it is important that the visual recognition be placed in an easy-to-find location on the Web page. For example, a medical clinic is named for a legacy gift of an individual, the top left corner of each Web page will typically show a revised logo of the medical clinic that includes the name of the donor. This style of naming rights recognition is what has come to be seen as an acceptable form in both the private and nonprofit sectors.

Many universities with fundraising campaigns feature an easy-to-find link to the campaign Web page displayed prominently on the home page of their Web sites. These campaign-specific Web pages can be described as another example of advanced donor relations. For examples, see the list later in this chapter.

Using dedicated Web pages to promote current fundraising campaigns can be seen as one of the advanced fundraising techniques. Organizations that employ these strategies and best practices for campaign Web sites are among the leaders in this sector.

Unfortunately, this technique is not commonly used by all other nonprofit organizations. When a nonprofit makes it difficult for a Web site visitor to find a link to the foundation Web page, it compromises its relationship to the potential donor.

Here are some of the residual benefits that I see coming from implementing advanced donor relations strategies:

- Enhance the brand name of the nonprofit.
- Promote the mission and vision of the organization.
- Enable "quiet conversations" with donors.
- Extend storytelling.

Discussing the nature and extent of online naming rights recognition is an advanced donor relations tactic that is coming into play more often. How the donor is recognized on the nonprofit's Web site is factoring into the wording of the naming rights agreement with greater frequency.

Nonprofits are leveraging their investment in their Web sites as they cherry-pick the advanced fundraising techniques that best suit their own situation. The beauty of the Internet is that the digital platform, the nonprofit's electronic billboard, is designed with a collapsible structure that lets you make incremental changes quickly and efficiently.

NAMING RIGHTS IN THE CAMPAIGN WEB SITE

A growing number of nonprofits are expanding the content of their Web sites with details about their fundraising efforts, be it in-campaign or not. For example, one long-standing practice has been the use of the Web site to advertise and promote endowment gifts, something that many universities do now.

What about using the Web site to promote and advertise the ask amounts for other named properties, such as interior spaces and locations, along with departments and existing buildings? This is another area of advanced fundraising techniques that appears to be gathering momentum. Think about it. You are in a competitive market. The campaign goal is in the millions, perhaps hundreds of million of dollars. Telling a story is a big part of what you do. If you could add depth to the story of the campaign goals and objectives, would you?

A growing number of nonprofits are choosing to do just that. They are adding the ask amounts for their naming opportunities to their campaign

Web pages, as well as information about named gifts already received.

What does that do for the Web site visitors? How does that change their online experience? What does it say about the nonprofit organization? How does that change the nature of the next conversation between the major gift donor prospect and the development staff? Naming rights strategies open a lot of doors. Which doors, and how many you open, are up to you.

Each of these questions in the above paragraph and throughout the book are offered in a rhetorical context. They are meant to get you thinking about the process, the strategies and related tactics that you use or don't use, regarding naming rights. There are no perfect answers, only a series of choices to be considered. If you find this approach perplexing I do not apologize; it's meant to get you thinking about how and why your organization makes the choices that it does.

Two techniques are used for sharing information about naming rights:

1. Shopping list approach
2. Descriptive text approach

Shopping List Approach

This technique is quickly becoming the most popular with nonprofits that want to share the ask amounts for naming rights with their donor community. Here is an example:

Name the Building	$5,000,000
Atrium	$2,500,000 — Named
Auditorium	$1,000,000
Stage in Auditorium	$500,000
Conference/Board Room	$350,000
Meeting Room (3) each	$100,000
Elevator	$75,000 — Named
Reception Area	$50,000
Administration Office	$25,000 — Named
Mail Room	$15,000
Garden Area	$10,000 — Named
Bench (5) each	$1,000

The shopping list approach allows people to view a collection, sometimes all, sometimes just a partial list, of naming opportunities. By posting this information on the Web site, a nonprofit can show a running scoreboard of what naming rights are available, and what naming gifts have already been received. The dollar values listed are typically the minimum amounts being asked in exchange for the naming rights to a designated property.

A shopping list like the one above usually has contact information nearby, so the Web site visitor knows who to call for more information.

Descriptive Text Approach

This technique for listing naming opportunities offers a description of the property or endowment property. Listings vary widely in style, ranging from a few words to several paragraphs complete with photographs of the property including artist drawings for new buildings or other facilities. Some nonprofit groups include detailed floor plans on their Web pages, allowing the major gift prospects to view the room, identify its location in the building, and learn the dimensions and details of what will be in the proposed named space. Here is an example of a descriptive text listing:

Cancer Institute—Career Development Physician

An endowment gift to the Career Development Physician Fund will enable the Cancer Institute to recruit and retain the best and brightest minds in our field. With a $3,000,000 gift, you can establish a permanent fund for an up-and-coming physician who will be pursuing new ways to treat, cure, and ultimately prevent cancer.

Other examples of the descriptive text approach are often used for a premiere naming opportunity, such as establishing a named scholarship fund or naming a facility that hasn't yet been constructed. Both techniques help to paint the picture for the major gift prospect in a manner that helps them to better understand the needs of the organization.

NAMING RIGHTS POLICY STATEMENTS

The topic of naming rights policies will be covered in depth in Chapter 6, "The Manager's Toolbox for Naming Rights."

As far as Internet naming rights, policy statements paint with a wide brush and generally include the Internet in with all other forms of signage and communications. Naming policies have been under the microscope due to the surge in major gift giving. Nonprofit organizations large and small have turned to these internal documents to assist in the named gift process. It is no longer acceptable to do things a certain way merely because that's the way it has been done for years. Given the high dollar amounts of major gifts and the importance of maintaining ongoing relationships with the donors, a consistent naming policy should be demanded—and applied.

During my research efforts, three nonprofit organizations offered insights and access to their own naming policies to aid in the discussion. Special thanks are due to Karen Whitehead at the University of Pittsburgh; Kathy Ruvolo at the University of California, Irvine; and Greg Shepherd, Executive

Vice President of Constituent Relations at the University of Washington in Seattle.

Universities such as these three have developed comprehensive naming policies that allow the development and donor relations staff to have meaningful and comprehensive discussions with major gift donors.

IMPLEMENTING ADVANCED DONOR RELATIONS TACTICS

During my survey, I was surprised by how many development staff announced that publicizing the ask amounts of naming opportunities is something they don't do and that they would not even consider it. That's interesting.

The Internet evolves in style and content every hour of every day. Nonprofit organizations that use Web sites to promote their naming opportunities appear to be a step ahead of groups that do not. Going one step farther and adding the ask amounts for naming opportunities helps both the Web site visitors and the development staff.

Web site visitors who take the time to go to your fundraising campaign Web pages have an interest in what you do. They are predisposed to finding out more about what you are doing. Campaign Web pages help do that. Best practices suggest that it is not only appropriate but expected to have easy-to-find links for online giving and planned giving. In each of those areas, the Web site visitor is offered more information about the fundraising effort and, in many cases, prompted to act now or at the very least to contact a development staff person for more information.

Why not take the same approach with naming rights and naming opportunities?

For groups that are concerned that publishing the ask amounts of naming opportunities on their Web site somehow compromises their fundraising efforts, I would say that's a spurious correlation. By that I mean that the people who visit a campaign Web site are interested in *your* organization. They may or may not be donors. But they have a genuine interest in finding out more information. Stewardship efforts, either implied or direct, helped to get that person to visit your campaign Web site in the first place. There is already some level of relationship. Going the extra mile and publishing the ask amounts merely shares information that may help to move that individual to the next step of making a major gift.

I suggest to you that donors know what is going on in the major gift marketplace better than the development staff. Research efforts by groups including the Association for Professional Fundraisers (AFP) suggest that major gift donors typically make gifts to six to eight nonprofit organizations. The quality of your relationship with major gift donors can be enhanced by offering more information, more data, and more numbers about major gift opportunities.

We live in a time when donors expect greater accountability, a greater degree of disclosure of information, and in-depth reporting after the major gift has been made.

LEGACY GIFT NAMING RIGHTS

When a donor makes a legacy gift, there is usually a donor agreement that outlines the extent and nature of the naming rights. For purposes of this discussion, think about a legacy gift that would name a school within a university, such as a school of business, law, engineering, social work, or other academic discipline within the university. Also note that there are two distinct types of legacy gifts: an endowment gift, and a gift specifically for the construction of a new facility.

In both cases, a donor agreement that spells out the nature of the commitment by the university and how the funds will be used is in place. I am referring to gift agreements where the naming rights are passed along in perpetuity as compared to limited term gifts. Gift agreements are typically drawn up on a case-by-case basis, and the wording is most often handled by the legal counsel to the institution.

The naming rights portion of the gift agreement includes all signage and written and online communication. Reprinting departmental business cards, stationery, and letterhead and changing the name of the school on the university's Web site is all part of the transition process of the naming rights associated with a legacy gift.

One other online tribute that has become standard practice is an online Web page dedicated to telling the history of the legacy gift donor. The hyperlink to the tribute Web page is generally found on the home page of the school and includes one or more photos of the donor(s), the history of their involvement, and some background details about them. Husband and wife donors quite often share in making the legacy gift, something that may or may not be reflected in the new name to the facility. The nice part about the online tribute page is its staying power and potential influence on future major gift donors.

INTERNET AND CORPORATE NAMING RIGHTS WITH NONPROFITS

An area that shows dynamic growth potential is how corporate naming rights are extended to the Web site of the nonprofit organization.

In most cases, the nonprofit organization uses a dedicated Web page that features the list of corporate sponsors ranked in order of sponsorship level. Because a Web page scrolls from top to bottom, as compared to a left-to-right in hard copy publications, typically one format is used to recognize the sponsors. The largest corporate sponsor(s) are listed at the top of the page and they usually get to display a larger logo than the second level, third level, and so on down the list. It's like an inverted pyramid where the title or lead sponsor gets the greatest amount of exposure by being listed at the top of the sponsorship list.

When online sponsorships first started to catch on, the sponsor's logo was almost always linked back to a feature Web page selected by the corporate sponsor. The click-through exposure that came from being listed on the nonprofit's sponsorship Web page helped to give a new dimension to the corporate sponsor. More exposure, more bang for the buck. In today's marketplace, not every nonprofit offers this type of an online naming rights benefit to the sponsor. It is a competitive advantage that can be used in your marketing material and in face-to-face discussions with sponsors.

Online naming rights recognition is just part of the overall sponsorship recognition package. The typical form of online naming rights recognition is for the company to provide an icon, usually one that is symbolic of brand name, and that icon is situated on the Web page to distinguish the corporate sponsorship of the event. Web site visitors can scroll over the corporate logo and with a click of the mouse drill down to a designated Web page of the corporate sponsor.

Depending on the size and the duration of the event, other Internet-related naming rights perks may be included, such as the following:

- Pre-event recognition in press releases
- "About the Company" reference to the company's Web site
- Onsite signage including company's URL
- Option to conduct onsite attendee product surveys
- Marketing rights associated with the event
- Inclusion in paid advertising campaign
- Opportunities to develop a contact database
- Corporate booth with giveaways noting Web site
- Media exposure, including billboards, display advertising, radio, etc.
- VIP reception
- Corporate table at the event

Depending on the corporate sponsor and how much they use their Web site in their marketing campaign, the naming rights benefits from corporate sponsorship can be quite substantial. At the end of the day, it's good for both the business and the nonprofit.

ONLINE SEARCH TIPS FOR TRACKING NAMING RIGHTS

When doing your own online searching for background details, here are a few tips to save you some time and effort:

- *Start by using Google.com, then expand to other search engines, including AltaVista.com, Yahoo.com, DogPile.com, etc.* Google search results continue to have the largest collection of data on topics such as naming opportunities. However, no one search engine can keep up with *all* the entries made on a daily basis; that's why you want to include at least two other search engines.

- *Use the same search criteria from search engine to search engine.* Changing simple search parameters can have a dramatic impact on your search results. Using a search such as "naming opportunities," with quotation marks will search for that specific phrase, whereas searching without quotation marks will search for instances of the separate words. Needless to say, the two searches yield very different results. Not using quotation marks reduces specificity and yields different, lower-quality information.

- *Use qualifying search parameters.* Examples include:
  - "naming opportunities" university
  - "naming opportunities" university 2008
  - "naming opportunities" university business 2008 named endowment 2008

  You can add additional search criteria to get countless variations. Including the name of a field of study, such as medicine, business, engineering, computer science, journalism, nursing, or others, will help tighten up a search somewhat. The more search elements you place inside the quotation marks, the narrower your search results will be. By adding or deleting one search word at a time, you can fine-tune your online search.

- Use specific keywords to target a sector or topic, such as:
  ○ school district or naming rights
  ○ parish or church "giving opportunities" stewardship

Different groups within the nonprofit sector use different words to describe what is basically the same thing. School districts typically refer to "selling naming rights," whereas universities or colleges seldom use the terms "sell" or "sold" when mentioning the subject of naming or giving opportunities at their institution. At the end of the day, though, they are all competing in the same marketplace.

TOP 10 WEB SITES FOR MARKETING NAMING RIGHTS

1. UCLA—A pioneer of the billion-dollar campaign, began in 1995
2. University of Michigan
3. Brown University—Use of campaign video
4. Dartmouth College—Extensive shopping list for review

5. University of Arkansas—Campaign wrap-up, including report in PDF

6. University of Oregon—Named leadership gifts

7. University of Chicago—Brand-name approach to campaign

8. University of Pittsburgh—Campaign charts, impact report

9. University of Virginia—One of the first $4-billion campaigns

10. Old Dominion University—Libraries pledge care with shopping list

UNIVERSITY BUYS STADIUM NAMING RIGHTS: INDIRECT BENEFITS OF AN INTERNET PRESENCE

On February 3, 2008, Super Bowl Sunday for the National Football League, the game between the New England Patriots and the New York Giants was broadcast around the world. The estimated viewing audience was around 93 million people, the third-highest for any television broadcast ever.

This year's Super Bowl has added interest for those in the nonprofit community because of where the football game is being played. It's a football stadium, but not just any football stadium. Super Bowl 42 was played at the University of Phoenix Stadium, a marvelous example of strategically acquired naming rights.

On September 25, 2006, the naming rights deal was announced. The University of Phoenix, one of the largest advertisers on the Internet, had no previous sports marketing deal in place prior to signing this agreement. The University and the Phoenix Cardinals of the NFL, host to Super Bowl 42, signed a 20-year $154-million naming rights contract. At $7.7 million per year, this was the second-highest naming rights fee per year for any NFL team at the time. Coincidentally, the New England Patriots, one of the contestants in the 2008 game, currently holds the top spot with a $300-million, 30-year naming rights deal with Gillette. The Washington Redskins' $7.6-million deal to name FedEx Field ranks third.

More important than the money, however, is that this deal is the first time a professional sports team from any league signed a naming rights deal with an educational institution. Although the University of Phoenix is not a nonprofit organization (it is owned by the Apollo Group Inc., a publicly traded company on the NASDAQ stock exchange), it has approximately 250,000 students, most working adults, enrolled in its distance education programs.

Going after the naming rights to a pro football stadium was an interesting play. The executives of the University of Phoenix would have already known that the Super Bowl game for 2008 had been awarded to that stadium. They had a game plan and executed it brilliantly. Company president John Sperling, who was 82 years old at the time of the naming rights deal, appears to have pulled off one of the most remarkable marketing coups of all time with this strategy.

This is an intriguing example that shows how a naming rights deal delivered a built-in national and international advertising campaign. It is difficult to estimate the dollar amount of the boost to the University of Phoenix brand name for the on-air mentions of the name, including coverage by traditional newspapers, radio, and television, before the event, on the day of the event, and during the post-game coverage. Oh, and don't forget all the DVDs and other electronic storage versions of the Super Bowl, which will continue to circulate among sports enthusiasts in the years to come. This typifies guerilla-style marketing at its best.

Even though the University of Phoenix is not a nonprofit institution, the link between professional sports and the higher education sector will have a crossover impact on naming rights deals with other universities in the future.

CORPORATE SPONSORSHIPS OF UNIVERSITY ATHLETICS LEVERAGE BRAND NAME

Corporate sponsors have learned to get the most bang for their sponsorship dollars by extending their brand name to the Web sites of the nonprofit group in which they have invested their dollars. Athletic departments have been able to show corporate partners credible evidence that validates their financial support. Web site–tracking software can provide details on the click-through numbers of visitors to athletic department Web pages and the subsequent drilling-down to corporate Web sites.

The use of sponsorship dollars is trying to achieve several things. First, the sponsor wants to raise the brand name awareness of its products and catch the eye of potential new consumers. Second, the sponsor wants to deepen its relationship with existing customers by showing its financial support to specific schools.

The typical athletic department "corporate partners" Web page has five to ten color images of the corporate logo that are hyperlinked to a designated Web page of the sponsor. As with all things, the more substantial the level of financial support, the greater the marketing exposure for the corporate sponsor.

One of the most important elements for a corporate sponsor is the demographic overlap between the members of the nonprofit organization and the products and services of the corporate sponsor. As you look around the Internet to see which companies are choosing to get involved with online naming rights, you will find that most sponsors fall into one of the following categories:

- ❖ Financial services companies, including banks, insurance providers, and retirement planning and wealth management
- ❖ Hospitals, healthcare, and cancer treatment centers
- ❖ Technology companies for computers, cell phones, and other wireless communication devices
- ❖ Food and beverages, including local pizza and fast food outlets
- ❖ Airlines and car rental

~ 4 ~

Legacy Gifts in a Nanosecond Society

> People make large gifts because they want to make a difference, not because of the naming rights that come with it.
>
> *Greg Sheridan, Executive Vice President*
> *for Constituent Relations,*
> *University of Washington, Seattle*

According to Greg Sheridan, donors don't make major gifts specifically for the naming rights that come with them. They make major gifts because they are passionate about the institution and they want to make a difference.

I asked Sheridan to identify some of the biggest changes he has seen in the named gift area. "The digital world has ensured a higher level of transparency," said the Seattle-based fundraising executive.

The Internet allows donors to drill down into a Web site and find out what's going on right across a nonprofit organization. With a few clicks of the mouse, the prospective donor can go from home page to front-page news items stored in the non-profit's online library. They can check into the latest research projects, the academic pursuits of faculty and students, medical research, or an upcoming special event.

Today's fundraising efforts are framed within the context of a digital world where everyone is busy, but you can reach out and touch someone just about anywhere, anytime. The trends all point to a greater emphasis on digital relationships with donors.

Sheridan offered other insights about legacy gift donors. For example, we talked about how fundraising used to be seen "as a contact sport," compared to today. In earlier times, a nonprofit organization would strategically arrange to put their best people in the room with a donor to pursue the ask. The emphasis was on the personal rapport, the story-telling, the ability to engage the donor and to listen for those precious insights that revealed the donor's passion or pet projects.

In the digital world, nonprofit organizations have to rely on electronic communications to a much greater degree. E-mail contacts are no longer relegated to a simple "I just wanted to say hi!" type of contact with donors. Sheridan noted that an increasing number of qualifying contacts, the kind that used to be done face-to-face, are compressed into a few lines of an e-mail to a major gift prospect. The big-picture stuff comes later.

Development staff have learned to be concise in their e-mail messages and have been schooled in the art of timely digital follow-ups. Wireless devices such as the ubiquitous Blackberry—which can store 500 e-mail contacts and phone numbers, provide mobile Internet access, and also serve as a telephone—have become standard issue for major gift staff. Gone are the days when every major gift request included a two- or three-page hard-copy proposal produced on quality paper and packaged in an expensive case. It's all going digital, baby—point, click, type, and send.

INTO THE DIGITAL LOOKING GLASS

As Greg Sheridan and so many other development professionals can attest, major gift donors have a passion for philanthropy, a passion for an organization, or in the case of the university, a passion for an academic institution. Philanthropists want to make a difference. They give of their time and their financial resources. The naming rights that come along with a major gift are often secondary.

So what is so special about making a named gift? When you talk to major gift donors before and even after they have decided to make the gift, they generally say that it's nice that they have been recognized by the nonprofit organization. But when you watch the donors later on, as they tour the facility with the new signage bearing the donor's name, you can see the pride in the way that they walk and hear the satisfaction in their voice as they tell their story to friends and family, describing why they chose to make a gift here, to leave their mark for others.

Perhaps it is as simple as that: modesty and pride of purpose, knowing that one person can make a difference.

ELECTRONIC COMPRESSION OF NAMING RIGHTS

Our Internet world appears to have some intriguing side effects in the field of naming rights gifts. It's a given that we all feel the effects of a lifestyle that is faster-paced than it was just a decade ago. But let's extend our thinking about the electronic compression of philanthropy and how that plays out with naming rights.

Follow this example through, and see if you can find some comparisons with your own organization.

You pick up your e-mail of the local news broadcast on your iPod or Blackberry, or maybe you even have a moment to catch the six o'clock news. Mr. and Mrs. XYZ just made a $25 million donation to the local university. The news item features a video clip of the ribbon-cutting ceremony, with lots of smiles and handshakes of congratulations all around. The story concludes by mentioning that the nonprofit has named the facility in honor of the donor. Nice.

That would have been the extent of it, 10 years ago: a fleeting moment of public acknowledgement in which people outside the immediate circle of friends and stakeholders heard about the naming rights gift. If we use the analogy of the stone tossed into the pool of water, this naming rights event would cause few ripples.

Fast-forward to 2008. We have a much larger ripple effect, because of the Internet and the shift toward more electronic communication. The traditional news media may want to hook up with the university via its online video announcement, instead of sending a reporter and photographer on site. The press release itself may go out to a much wider audience, via e-mail and a subsequent HTML newsletter, in which the naming gift may be the feature of the month.

To that we can add the digital archive of the naming rights gift, which will stay on the university's Web site for years to come. All naming gifts stories go into the news archive, which is accessed by other members of the donor community. The press release stories often share direct quotes from the donor about why he or she made the gift, and the passion and the vision he or she has for the institution. These press releases generally offer background about the individual and his or her long-standing relationship with the institution.

Something I noticed as I read through more than a thousand of these types of announcements is the naming gift track record shared in the story. It's not uncommon, when we hear about a top-tier gift of $25 million or more, to find that the donor previously made a named endowed scholarship gift or a generous contribution that established a center of learning or other property that has been named in their honor. The big gift of $25 million is a continuation of the donor's long-standing support and philanthropic enthusiasm for the institution.

Now let's think about the size of the stone tossed into the digital pool, the size of the splash, and how long this single splash will resonate for donors, today and in the future.

NAMING RIGHTS RIPPLE FORWARD IN TIME

The announcement of a major gift can have an intoxicating effect on the people involved in and around a nonprofit organization. There is a wow and a buzz that goes through the office, is shared in telephone conversations, and brings smiles to people's faces and twinkles to their eyes. It's magical.

I suggest that naming rights gifts can have a ripple effect on the donor community, who may first learn of a gift months, maybe years later. They learned about it because they were searching the Internet for information on the nonprofit or on the donor. Maybe they knew the donor personally or simply knew of them; maybe they have an enthusiasm for the nonprofit. The ease of use and the accessibility of the Internet, helped by the nonprofit's archive of press releases or its Web page honoring donors, provides the information—an archived story from 15 months ago, a Web page celebrating the named gift —that may rekindle a desire to help the nonprofit.

The digital reach of the Internet is far greater than we can easily calculate and sometimes even imagine. I suggest that the naming rights gifts of recent years will continue to resonate for many years to come.

BILLION-DOLLAR CAMPAIGN LEGACY GIFT OPPORTUNITIES

The billion-dollar fundraising campaigns going on across the country feature a wide array of legacy gift opportunities. In the pages that follow, you can browse through the list of one such fundraising campaign at the University of Pittsburgh.

As with many contemporary campaigns, the university found that they far exceeded the initial fundraising goal sooner than expected. As a result, the leadership of the university extended the financial target. The University of Pittsburgh is on its way to over $2 billion in the current campaign.

Fundraising efforts like this feature campus-wide gift-giving opportunities. Donors like to know they are making a difference. A growing university has many areas of need. Naming opportunities and the naming right recognition that comes with them help to match the needs of the donor to the needs of the university.

Examples from the University of Pittsburgh 2008 Naming Opportunities

Exhibits 4.1, 4.2, and 4.3 feature a glimpse into some of the current naming opportunities at the University of Pittsburgh. You will find examples of

EXHIBIT 4.1 University of Pittsburgh School of
                 Engineering

Facilities	Ask Amounts
School of Engineering	$30 million
Benedum Auditorium	$5 million
Manufacturing Assistance Center	$2 million
Microfabrication Laboratory	$1 million
Benedum Lobby	$1 million
Undergraduate Tutoring Center	$500,000
Digital Classroom	$500,000
Mixed Technology Microsystems Lab	$500,000
Departmental Research Lab	$500,000
Undergraduate Measurement Lab	$250,000
Enhanced Learning Classrooms	$200,000
Dean's Suite	$200,000
Virtual Enterprise Lab	$150,000
Electronics Lab	$100,000
Signal Processing Lab	$100,000
Departmental Suites	$100,000
Departmental Conference Room	$50,000
Student Organizations Office	$25,000

EXHIBIT 4.1 (Continued)

Endowments	Ask Amounts
Endowed Chair	$2 million to $3 million
Professorship	$2 million
Faculty Fellows	$500,000 to $1 million
Scholarship	$150,000 to $250,000

EXHIBIT 4.2 University of Pittsburgh School of Dental Medicine

Facilities	Ask Amounts
School of Dental Medicine	$25 million
Clinical Skills Laboratory	$500,000
Student Lounge	$150,000
Museum Expansion	$100,000
Clinical Skills Laboratory Pod	$10,000
Endowments	**Ask Amounts**
Endowed Chair	$2 million to $3 million
Professorships	$2 million
Scholarships	$250,000 to $750,000
Student Awards	$10,000 to $150,000

(Continued)

EXHIBIT 4.2 (Continued)

Programmatic	Ask Amounts
Name a Division	$1 million
Research	$500,000 to $1 million
Name a Department	$500,000

EXHIBIT 4.3 University of Pittsburgh Cancer Institute

Naming Opportunities	Ask Amounts
Named Department	$3 million
Endowed Chair, Clinical Research	$1 million
Endowed Chair, Basic Research	$1 million
Research Labs, each	$1 million
Clinical Labs, each	$1 million
Endowed Faculty Fellowship	$500,000
Endowed Post-Doctoral Fellowship	$500,000
Endowed Research Fellowship	$250,000
Named Endowed Fund	$50,000

The University of Pittsburgh Office of Institutional Advancement Named Facilities and Programs Policy is contained in the Appendix.

academic need ranging from naming a school to scholarship and program endowments. The dollar figures shown are the minimum ask amounts.

I would like to acknowledge the support of my research by the University of Pittsburgh in allowing their information to be published here for your review. For more background details, I refer you to the University of Pittsburgh Office of Institutional Advancement Named Facilities and Programs Policy, which can be found in the Appendix.

~ 5 ~

Naming Rights and Endowment Gifts

The naming rights that accompany endowment gifts have been taking on new meaning in the past few years. A large number of first-time donors have been stepping up and making million-dollar gifts, endowment gifts to be exact, for programs, scholarships, and, more recently, designated areas of interest in healthcare.

Endowments have unique attributes, unlike the naming opportunities for bricks and mortar buildings. I give a tip of the hat to donors who get involved in capital campaigns with their charitable support. Thousands of lobbies, staircases, auditoriums, conference rooms, administrative suites, classrooms, surgery rooms, and hallways have been named in their honor.

But endowment gifts, well, are kind of special. Why? Compound interest.

Remember high school math class, when you worked with present value and future value formulas? Neither do I, to tell the truth, but I do remember one lesson that came out of those study periods: money doubles every seven years when invested at an annual rate of 7% interest. Nice.

Endowment gifts are a different type of discussion between development staff and prospective donor. The handful of colleges and universities that have been marketing endowment gifts for over a century can attest to the benefits of this type of named gift; see the list below. Named endowed funds typically start at $25,000 for the larger universities and colleges and $10,000 for smaller institutions of higher education.

University Endowments Over $5 Billion—2007 Estimates	Billion $
Yale University	$22.5
Stanford	$17.2
Princeton University	$15.8
University of Texas	$15.6
Massachusetts Institute of Technology	$9.9
Columbia University	$7.1
University of Michigan	$7.0
University of California	$6.7
Northwestern University	$6.6
University of Pennsylvania	$6.6
Texas A&M	$6.5
University of Notre Dame	$6.5
University of Chicago	$6.0

Duke University	$5.9
Washington University in St. Louis	$5.6
Cornell	$5.4
Emory University	$5.0
University of Virginia	$5.0

Source: Dig In Research 2007 Inc., *National Survey of Naming Opportunities*

CRUNCH THE NUMBERS, ENJOY THE CASH FLOW

The most common endowment fund is one that is set up in perpetuity. When a donor makes an endowment gift, the money goes into a designated endowment fund. The principle amount is not touched; annual payouts come from the interest earned. Named funds have become extremely popular with the donor community.

In the January 2008 issue of the *Gazette*, published by the University of North Carolina, the development team touted the closure of the Carolina First Campaign, a multiyear effort that raised more than $2.3 billion. The results included the following:

New endowed professorships	208
New merit- and need-based scholarships	577
Number of donors	193,000

(Continued)

Alumni gift	36%
Corporations and foundations	38%
Friends and others	26%

The results from the University of North Carolina campaign are outstanding. When you try to raise more than $2 billion, a lot of the money comes in the form of endowment gifts. What does that do for the university in the short and long term?

Aside from the obvious accomplishment of achieving the campaign goal, the university now has 193,000 donors with whom they can work, just from this campaign. When you look deeper into the numbers and pull out the figures for first-time donors of more than $1 million, it gets really interesting. All of those $1-million donations were recognized as named gifts. The naming rights bestowed on the first-time million-dollar donors, in particular, help to create a bond between the person and the place. The donors now have a financial attachment to the institution, driven by an emotional urge to draw closer, to become involved. It's an important threshold to cross in the process of evaluating the capacity to give, and a key stepping stone along the path of moves management philosophy practices.

Moves management is an organized approach to developing the relationships with donors and prospects. From the first time a donor makes a gift, the methodology employed to thank the donor and the subsequent stewardship efforts to move that donor through the pipeline of fundraising opportunities can be considered as moves management activities. A gift to the annual campaign may be followed by a larger gift the following year at which time the development staff begin to move the donor towards major gift or planned gift-giving opportunities. The larger the gifts, the more personalized attention the donor receives from the nonprofit organization as it works to determine capacity and interest by the donor in making additional gifts.

Major gifts that result in the transfer of naming rights to the donor are an example of when the moves management strategies and tactics become more obvious. This may include one-on-one meeting or thank you luncheon with the chief executive of the nonprofit organization or a joint reception that involves a large number of major gift donors. The dollar amount that qualifies as a major gift varies from nonprofit to nonprofit and so does the style and type of moves management activities. Naming rights are secondary to the philanthropic commitment to offer financial support. But I suggest that the naming rights are a treasured legacy, if only within one's heart. The long-term potential for future named gifts dramatically increases in direct correlation to the number of lower-level gifts received from the most recent campaign.

Naming endowments after the people who donate is a perk that comes with the territory. Moves management tactics and strategies will determine which donors become more involved in the future. Stewardship is the key.

THE HISTORY OF THE ENDOWED CHAIR

The endowed chair has a rich tradition spanning five centuries. How did this tradition begin, you ask? We have to turn the pages of history to Oxford University, in the year 1502, when Margaret of Richmond, mother of Henry VII, established the Lady Margaret Professorship of Divinity. In 1721, Harvard College established the first endowed chair in America, the Hollis Professorship of Divinity. Both are still in existence today.

For universities and colleges, the endowed chair brought a flexibility to the revenue stream that allowed diversity in the curriculum, support and retention of professors, and financial assistance to students.

Today, endowed chairs continue the traditions begun long ago. Financial support touches the lives of people in courses of study not even dreamed of even 20 years ago. From genetics to global security, from nanotechnology to information literacy, from bioinformatics to urban education, the list is long and growing.

During the winter of 2008, a remarkable number of naming rights announcements were made, tumbling one on top of another. The price tags for endowed chairs rose higher, faster than the price of gasoline at the pumps. Universities and colleges of all sizes have been revamping their naming policies in the midst of fundraising campaign kickoffs. One of the first things to review is the ask amounts for endowed chairs. The next is the number and type of endowed chairs to be offered.

Not that long ago, you would have had to do an extensive search to find ask amounts above the $1-million mark outside of national universities. In today's marketplace, that number is quickly being replaced as multiple endowed chair properties slot into the marketing mix of the fundraising campaign.

An endowed chair is not just about growing the academic offerings or supporting students; it's about the economic impact on the bottom line, creating jobs, developing centers of excellence, and staying one step ahead of the competition.

When UCLA closed the books on its record-breaking $3-billion campaign, the school raised the bar for the entire nonprofit sector and left an indelible mark on the fundraising landscape. Completed billion-dollar fundraising campaigns at the University of Arkansas, the University of Michigan, and the University of North Carolina have kept the momentum going.

Gifts to endowed chairs have become an integral part of the new era in campaign strategy. When the moves management philosophy is applied to the equation, it suggests that securing a gift for an endowed chair dramatically increases the likelihood of subsequent major gifts or a planned gift at a later date.

Stepping back to try to glimpse the big picture, we can see other dynamics at work. Competitive advantage, for one, is at the forefront of discussions by the board of governors as they look to push the envelope and enhance the position of their school. Why? Perhaps these are a few of the underlying motivations:

- The pursuit of sponsored research projects
- Retention of educators and staff
- Recruiting the top-of-class students

AN ENDOWED CHAIR IS A VALUABLE PROPERTY

Thanks to the generous support of donors and the creative marketing efforts of development professionals, the bar has been raised for what it takes to endow a chair at an academic institution.

> May 26, 2006, Clemson University—The $10 million endowed chair, created by $5 million from the state matched by $5 million from other sources, will support a world-renowned scholar, two junior faculty positions, and funds for researchers to complement existing research.

Announcements about matching gifts for endowments, like the one from Clemson University, resonate within the local and national fundraising community. Thanks to Clemson and to the nonprofit sector as a whole, the bar has shifted a little bit higher. At a time when we are witnessing an enormous transfer of wealth from one generation to the next, high-profile gifts like the $10-million endowed chair at Clemson stretch the blue sky thoughts of donors and development staff alike.

Recent naming rights bestowed on endowment gifts

- February 11, 2008—Peter and Sally Kay donated $2 million to endow a professorship in clinical cancer research at Purdue University.
- February 7, 2008—UCLA announced the Pete Kameron Endowed Chair in Law in appreciation of a gift of $1.5 million.
- January 31, 2008—Rainbow Babies and Children's Hospital in Cleveland, Ohio, received $1 million from the family of a former doctor to create an endowed chaired position in pediatric endocrinology.
- January 30, 2008—Western Kentucky University's Department of Engineering received $2 million to establish the Greulich Endowed Chair in Robotics and Automation Engineering
- January 30, 2008—Marquette University is asking $35 million for seven endowed chairs in the new engineering school. The Milwaukee-based university recently received $25 million towards the capital requirements of the project.

- January 28, 2008—University of Bridgeport, Connecticut, announced a $1-million gift to establish an endowed chair in chemistry.
- January 25, 2008—Penn State announced a $3-million gift for the Peter and Angela Dal Pezzo Department Head Chair of Industrial and Manufacturing Engineering

The list of charitable gifts to endow a chair for at least $1 million goes on and on. In a way, this is an affirmation of the work being done at colleges and universities across the country. Donors vote with their dollars. We can count this as another *yes* on the scorecard for supporting the pursuit of excellence and greater achievements in post-secondary education.

EMERGING TRENDS IN ENDOWED CHAIRS

The pace of change and the speed at which events are happening in our 24/7 world puts a lot of pressure on fundraisers to get it right. The endowed chair is in a way symbolic of the rapid changes we are experiencing in the fundraising world. In this chapter, we will examine some of the emerging trends, along with examples and analysis of why I think things are evolving as they appear to be. The top two emerging trends are diversifying the endowed chair and differentiating the endowed chair label in higher education.

Diversification of the Endowed Chair as a Naming Rights Commodity

By far the most significant trend is the way that the endowed chair has become a fundraising commodity offered outside higher education.

The words "endowed chair" can be seen on the naming opportunity lists across the country and around the world. From YWCAs to the local museum and art gallery, from hospitals to international environmental groups, there is an ever-widening group of nonprofit organizations using some variation of an endowed chair to promote their cause to donors.

Billions of dollars will continue to pour into higher education over the next decade, but at the same time there is a groundswell of activity competing for the attention of major gift donors. The trend of making six-, seven- and eight-figure endowed gifts is landing in a wider range of nonprofit bank accounts more than ever before, and momentum is continuing to build in that direction.

Part of this trend can be attributed to the high turnover of fundraising staff throughout the nonprofit sector. The people who worked on big campaigns at universities and colleges often move on to other nonprofits when the big push of the campaign is finished. They take with them the knowledge and understanding of how to market and promote an endowed chair. An ever-increasing number of nonprofits have begun to embrace this approach and fit the endowed chair into the marketing mix of naming opportunities.

For the most recent perspective on endowed chairs, I recommend you do a quick online search. Enter the search parameter using quotation marks at the beginning and end, press enter, and scan the results; you may be surprised at what you find.

HEALTHCARE

May 2, 2006—City of Hope Cancer Center, Los Angeles named the first holder of the newly endowed chair in information sciences, established with a gift of $2.5 million.

Teaching hospitals, with their links to universities, were some of the first to benefit from the expanding nature of the endowed chair. Given their close ties to the Medical School, the teaching hospitals must have represented a seamless crossover in the mind of the donor. An endowed chair in clinical research is an extension of other fundraising efforts going on within the university.

Similar examples of the ubiquitous nature of the endowed chair can be found at local libraries (curator positions), in medical research (clinical and surgical staff positions), and in an ever-widening list of key staff in other nonprofits.

Differentiation of the Endowed Chair in Higher Education

With so many campaigns on the go in the higher education sector, fundraising staff have been looking for other ways to compete for major gifts. Diversifying existing products is a marketing technique commonly used in the consumer and durable goods areas, such as televisions, computers, clothing, cars and trucks, airlines, and so on. In this scenario, you start with an existing product—in our example, the endowed chair—then add a variety of features to expand the initial product offering.

Airlines, for example, use the same planes to transport passengers from place to place, yet charge a higher fare for those who want the comfort and service that comes from sitting in first class or business class. No one gets there any sooner. But the experience of the trip can be greatly enhanced by sitting in the wide, very comfortable recliner with built-in TV in the third row, compared to the cramped space for those sitting in the back of the plane.

Development staff have learned to apply diversification strategies to their shopping list of naming opportunities for the endowed chair, partly in response to what other universities are doing, and partly in response to requests by donors, who see the diversification strategies in use elsewhere.

Higher-education donors have some unique attributes. One of those is the fact that many people completed an undergraduate degree from one university and then attended a second for a master's degree or other graduate studies. These people have multiple allegiances, some stronger than others. It is not uncommon for the same person to be solicited for a major gift from two universities at the same time.

This is where the diversification of the endowed chair began and is continuing today. Based on my national survey of naming opportunities, I have examined the labels used and the ask amounts associated with endowed chairs in higher education.

In the list below, you find 15 different labels or titles that are in use today for an endowed chair. Each one comes with a separate price tag for the minimum ask amount. In all cases, there is a financial hierarchy of price tags for the various endowed chairs at any one institution. A Chancellor's or President's endowed chair typically is the most expensive, followed by the Dean's endowed chair, then by department, then the faculty.

Diversification of the endowed chair as a commodity has added numerous levels above what once was a single named-gift tradition. Most importantly, donors have responded in robust fashion and appear to enjoy having a choice as to the type of endowment gift they can make and the way they can best target their financial support to an area that is of most interest to them.

As you review the list, think about the strategy that your own organization uses. To the right are dollar ranges in use for each type of endowed chair.

Chancellor's Endowed Chair	$4 million to $7 million
Presidential Endowed Chair	$4 million to $7 million
Regent's Endowed Chair	$3 million to $5 million

Trustees Endowed Chair	$2 million to $4 million
Distinguished Endowed Chair	$2 million to $5 million
Dean's Endowed Chair	$3 million to $5 million
Endowed Chair—Career Development	$1 million to $2 million
Renaissance Endowed Chair	$1 million to $2 million
Endowed Chair—Incremental	$1 million to $2 million
Named Faculty Endowed Chair	$1 million to $4 million
Special Interest Endowed Chair	$2 million to $4 million
Newly Established Faculty Endowed Chair	$1 million to $3 million
University Endowed Chair	$1 million to $3 million
Department Endowed Chair	$1 million to $3 million
Term Endowed Chair	$500,000 to $2 million
Endowed Chair	$1 million to $2.5 million

~ 6 ~

Manager's Toolbox for Naming Rights

The Manager's Toolbox offers effective processes for developing an inventory, examining related policy statements, and setting the ask amounts for naming rights. It was developed to assist nonprofit organizations to be in a more informed position to make strategic decisions.

Who is this for? Intermediate to senior management who are involved in the planning stages of fundraising campaigns. The process outlined here offers a starting point to help move you through this part of the overall campaign plan. Examples and discussion points offer insights about how to manage each stage of the process. Start with this outline and adapt it to suit the needs of your organization.

Naming Rights Checklist

- Conduct a Historic Named Gift Survey
- Review donor relations/stewardship activities and policies

- Develop the list of naming opportunities
- Review/develop the naming rights policy statement
- Research the marketplace and create benchmarks for ask amounts
- Review/develop the naming rights agreement
- Review/develop Web site strategy
- Learn the demographics
- Choose pricing strategies
- Celebrate leadership gifts

Selling naming rights has been equated to a financial windfall by many people these days. At a time when other sources of funding have dried up, the notion of jumping on the naming rights bandwagon appears to be a quick fix for the financial troubles faced by thousands of nonprofits.

Over the last decade nonprofits large and small have been the beneficiaries of named gifts. In 2007, I estimate that there were over $4 billion of named gifts made to American nonprofit organizations. Some of those named gifts came from donors who had long-standing relationships with the nonprofit, and the ask was something that had been cultivated over years. In other cases, the philanthropic gesture came as a surprise.

USING THE MANAGER'S TOOLBOX FOR NAMING RIGHTS

The objective of this chapter is to help you formulate a plan to sell naming rights to donors and sponsors. By applying a consistent approach and adding structure to your methodology, you will increase the likelihood of having naming opportunities that donors and sponsors will be interested in. This is not, however, a guarantee that you will close more naming rights agreements. The goal of this chapter is for the nonprofit organization to be in a more informed position to make strategic decisions about what to offer for sale and how much to ask for.

WORKING THROUGH THE NAMING RIGHTS CHECKLIST

As you work your way through the Manager's Toolbox you may want to have a pen and paper close at hand. Make some notes, and jot down ideas as they come to you. When you stay in the moment and allow your mind to swim through the possibilities, you are more likely to catch the rhythm of what is going on with your own campaign in relation to the ideas and concepts in this text.

Historic Named Gift Survey

Assumptions and Objectives. When you conduct a Historic Named Gift Survey, it is important to start out by stating the assumptions for conducting the survey. For example, a community college that is planning on the third expansion in the last twenty years could note that the survey will examine what properties have been added since the college opened. Or, they could use the assumption that they only want to examine named gifts from the last ten years. By setting out the assumptions, you help put into context the information that will be gathered during the survey.

This process does several things for your organization. For starters, there will be a current inventory of what has been named in the past. It would be helpful to know what has been named a philanthropic gift and if there are any honorary naming rights, especially for outside spaces or building and interior naming opportunities.

The information-gathering process will be helpful in establishing a framework of the dollar amounts given by funders in the past for major gifts. This will come in handy later on when you start working on setting the ask amounts for current naming opportunities.

You will need to have upper management's buy-in to support your efforts on this project. Thousands of dollars, in some cases millions in potential revenue, depend on upper management's support to see this through.

Once that is in place you are good to go. Pick up a clipboard with some sheets of paper and a pen to write with and be sure to have on some comfortable walking shoes. It's time to get a historical snapshot of what properties have been named. Knowing the past will help you to formulate a plan for your next campaign. Gather as much information as you can within a predefined time limit.

Set Minimum Dollar Amount for Survey.   Set a minimum dollar amount for the data you are looking for. The amount will vary depending on the size of the organization. In national universities and colleges you may only want to know about named gifts over $5 million. In a regional arts center, the data collection may be set at $1,000. Be consistent.

In larger organizations you will most likely need to enlist the help of staff members in other departments. Smaller nonprofits may borrow parts of the methodology used for larger groups, especially if you have satellite office locations.

Once you have the buy-in from upper management, establish a *target date(s)* for the information collection. For example, if you send out the request of information on the second of the month, ask to have it returned to you by the 10th of the same month. Let everyone know about the status of the survey and when the results will be made available to them. Give them and yourself a simple process to follow. Keep it simple. Include what to look for and offer a couple of examples. Use categories to group named gifts such as:

- Named buildings and outdoor spaces
- Named indoor spaces and facilities
- Named endowments

Use a separate data collection report for each unit. In higher education that would include each academic faculty, administrative department, facilities, and other groups. In a health-care facility

you could organize this by building or by department. For those nonprofits that have multiple offices
around the country, collect the naming data from
each branch office if you plan on running a national
campaign to attract local, regional, or national sponsors. In the following table, you will find a sample
form that can be adapted to suit your organization.

Categories for Grouping Named Gifts

Named building and outdoor space	Name of donor	What year	Dollar amount
John Smith Library	John Smith and family	1996	$1,000,000
MTS Credit Union Parking Garage	MTS Credit Union	2004	$250,000
Named indoor spaces			
Jones Atrium	Fred Jones	2005	$150,000
Pacini Staircase	Eddy and Ruth Pacini	2005	$50,000

Start by creating a blank table, similar to this
one, with four columns. The number of rows will
depend on how many items you want to include in
the list. A suggestion to help you accumulate the
data you want is to bring up the subject of doing a
Historic Named Gifts Survey as early in the discussion phase of a new campaign as possible. By letting
people know in advance (e.g., at staff meetings and
with e-mail follow ups) you may be able to cast a

wider net and dig up named gift details that will influence other stages in the planning process. The more data you collect in step one, the greater the impact on the strategic planning steps that come later.

Publish a Summary Report.   An important part about this stage is to make sure that an edited list of named gifts and current naming opportunities is made available to the person in charge of the faculty, department, or facility. If you ask for something be sure to give something back in return.

Once you have completed the data gathering survey you can now create a Historical Named Gifts Report. This will come in handy during the latter stages and will help get people thinking about what to include in the upcoming campaign.

Review Donor Relations/Stewardship Policies

Distinguishing Between Donor Relations and Steward-ship.   For the purposes of this book, I define donor relations as how a nonprofit says thank you for a gift made by a donor and works to cultivate new ones. My definition of stewardship is everything that happens after the gift has been made.

A review of current donor relations policies may reveal new opportunities to engage existing donors relative to the upcoming campaign. By examining the stewardship activities you may come across lapsed donors of major gifts; think of action plans for current donors and related ideas that you will be able to pass along in the campaign planning meetings.

How Do You Say "Thank You"? How do you say thank you to your donors? Having a clear understanding of the "thank you" process in your organization is important as you move forward towards the style and wording of "thank you" for major gifts that become a named property.

As you review the existing policy statement and current practices, think about how well the "thank you" efforts work in conjunction with the moves management objectives. When does an annual gift donor get handed off to become a major gift prospect or a planned giving prospect? How does the organization work with existing major gift donors who have supported the organization at dollar amounts just below and just above the minimum named gift level?

The crossover of donor relations and stewardship is often blurred, especially in small organizations where development staff has to wear several hats when they come to work.

As you review the "thank you" process, you will also want to review the hierarchy of sign-offs for thank you responses. Nonprofit organizations generally use an escalating ladder of sign-offs based on the dollar amount of the gifts. The larger the dollar amount, the more senior the staff person is who signs the "thank you" to the donor. By reviewing the hierarchy now, you could make adjustments in the process for named gifts from donors.

Thank You Campaign Preceded Billion Dollar Success. Stewardship efforts are often taken for granted and in many nonprofits are not always given serious attention. For those about to embark on a significant fundraising effort, I heartily suggest you rethink your approach.

One university I know of postponed the launch of a billion dollar campaign for a year when a major donor said no to a request for support. When asked why the request was denied, the donor told the vice president of development that they had no idea what the university had done with the money from the last gift. They were tired of being taken for granted.

For those of you who may have lived through a similar experience, you can attest to the awkward feeling of having to back out of the room while making apologies for others. The search for answers began moments later.

By the very action of saying "no," the donor decided to step forward and hold the university accountable. The donor's comments and refusal to make another gift came from their expectations for a stewardship report, if only on an occasional basis.

One of the emerging trends amongst major gift donors is the increasing expectations for high levels of accountability, reporting, and ongoing stewardship. The leadership of the university's development office realized that they had not done a good enough job in saying thank you to donors. Things needed to change. Change involved every member of the development office stopping their efforts in gift solicitation until the university had made the effort to say "thank you" to every single one of their existing donors. It was a dramatic step that took about a year to complete. The university then launched the campaign with a goal of $1 billion. It turned out to be the most successful one in the school's history.

Develop a List of Naming Opportunities

As you are asking people to find the historical data about previous named gifts, it is a good time to get them thinking about what naming opportunities— in their unit, faculty, department, or area—they would like to see in the upcoming campaign.

Carryover from the Last Campaign. Major gifts staff may already have donors interested in making a named gift as a carryover from the last campaign. As we move forward from the spring of 2008, it has become common practice to start planning the next capital campaign soon after the current one is completed. The nature of major gift solicitation has become extremely competitive. If your organization does not ask a qualified donor about making a named gift, there is a high probability that another one will.

Donors Like Something New. Developing a list of naming opportunities will vary from campaign to campaign. Those that include new buildings, new facilities, and new outdoor spaces, have been attracting the majority of interest from donors. Surveys show that donors have several hot buttons when it comes to supporting their charities of choice. Mission and vision is one followed closely by the need to feel like their donation is making a difference. When you begin to develop the list of naming opportunities, just focus on what you could include on the list, not how much to ask for.

If you have a new facility under construction take a walk through and look around, it will help you to visualize things. Talk to the architects about their vision for the end product. Talk to the dean of the school if this is in higher education, or the key members of a hospital staff, or the musicians who will be performing on stage in the new venue. Try to see the features and benefits of the new facility through the eyes of others. The list of naming opportunities may be easier to imagine when you do.

Buildings and Outside Spaces. To begin with, choose a starting point, which can be either indoors or outdoors. From the outside, you want to consider these naming opportunities:

- Naming the campus or grounds for the new campaign
- Naming the buildings individually
- Naming the roads if they are on private property
- Naming the environmentally friendly roof in whole or in part

- Naming the gardens
- Naming a parking facility
- Naming other designated outdoor spaces
- Naming a grove of trees or by tree, bench, walkway

Outdoor naming gifts typically are the largest of the campaign. If you have a building to name, consider including a dollar amount as an endowment to cover annual operating expenses.

Athletics and Recreation Facilities. For many universities and colleges, high schools, and other educational groups, the push to build new athletic facilities is near the top of the list. From football stadiums to hockey rinks to practice facilities that double as an inducement to attract new student-athletes to the academic support centers for varsity players, the range of naming opportunities has grown dramatically in recent years.

Ten years ago many institutions would have been happy to receive a naming gift for the stadium. Today the development staff has a more extensive list for donors to consider such as:

- Naming the entire athletic complex
- Naming the stadium or other primary facility
- Naming the field
- Naming the scoreboard
- Naming the units within the facility

- Naming Lockers, benches, offices, weight room, and others

With the popularity of athletics, some development staff are asking for a naming gift well above the traditional 50% of cost and getting it. Look for this trend to continue in the future.

Indoor Naming Opportunities. The inside of a building holds a wide assortment of potential naming opportunities. Your list will depend on the type of building and amount and size of spaces available, along with what is in the building. Last but not least in your consideration are what the building is used for and its location relative to the center or focal point of the organization. Suggestions for interior naming opportunities are offered below.

Many of these naming opportunities are common to many nonprofits regardless of the type of organization, including the main lobby and reception areas. Think of the lists as having transferable items. This may be a starting point as you develop your own list of naming opportunities.

Arts and Culture—Performing and Visual Arts

Lobby	Atrium
Reception area	Ticket booth
Auditorium	Box seats/premium
Seating by rows, area	seating area
Orchestra pit	Individual seating
Musical instruments	Conductor's platform
	Stage

(Continued)

Backstage area	Green room
Dressing rooms	Costume area/storage
Performance sponsor	Tour sponsor
Gallery sponsor	Exhibit sponsor

Administrative and Common Areas

Executive director's office	Other key staff offices
Elevators	Staircase
Stained glass windows	Entrance area
Board room	Conference room
Research area	Furniture
Small meeting rooms	Each floor of the
Staff lounge	building/wing
	Mail room

Education—Higher Education, Private Schools, High Schools, and School Boards

Dean's suite	Superintendent's office
Main lobby	Lobbies on other floors
Computer laboratory	Laboratory equipment
Academic programs	Academic departments

Endowed chairs: president, chancellor, trustee, dean, department, term, clinical/medical research, renaissance and others

Health Care/Hospitals

Medical research labs	Scientific research labs
Medical equipment—100% of cost	Operating rooms
	Emergency clinic
Medical care programs	
Emergency areas	
Staff retention/recruiting endowments	
Endowed chairs by area of specialization	

Hospital rooms/patient care rooms

Treatment facilities	Hospital wings
Cancer centers	Senior care facilities
Nurse's stations	Family rooms
Indoor gardens	Artwork collection

Naming Policy Statement

Your organization's naming policy statement is critically important prior to, during, and after your fundraising campaigns. Many nonprofits that did not have a written naming policy found themselves backed into a corner over naming rights. Thanks to the generosity of the University of Pittsburgh and the University of Washington, we have several documents of this type available for your in-depth analysis and review in the Appendix at the back of this book.

The universities who have shared their documents in the Appendix are both currently engaged in multibillion-dollar fundraising campaigns. Other nonprofits should be able to find information in these naming policy statements that they can relate to and that will help them work on their own documents.

I encourage groups that are in transition in their fundraising efforts to review the style and content, not just the words, in those documents. A naming policy statement, or any other for that matter, should be written to fit the organization. Some will be more elaborate than others. Here are some of the key areas to consider in your naming policy statement:

- General policy
- Buildings and outdoor properties
- Interior properties
- Endowment gifts
- Individual and family naming rights
- Corporate and organization naming rights
- Approval of naming rights gifts
- Recognition

General Policy. The general policy on naming rights establishes the ground rules for the properties that can be named. It may be only a few sentences long or may encompass several paragraphs. This section of a naming policy statement can include an overview of the classes of donors that the organization deem appropriate to make named gifts, describing the types of individuals, foundations, corporations, or other groups in the context of their relationship with the nonprofit organization.

The general policy is meant as qualifying criteria that can allow for wiggle room at some point in time in the future. The general policy may use expansive language to allow for broader interpretations of your organization's naming rights policy. For a more comprehensive discussion on this type of wording, it is best to consult with legal counsel.

In the higher education sector, for example, many universities include qualifying conditions regarding naming rights attached to gifts from corporate donors.

> Only in rare situations will a building or outdoor area be named for a corporation or organization whose gift represents a major contribution toward total project cost.
>
> From the University of Washington Facilities and Naming Policy, reprinted with the university's consent. (See the Appendix for the complete document.)

When you write your general policy statement, frame the context of the naming policy so that development staff understand what it means to make a named gift. Encourage discussions and plan for periodic review with senior members and volunteers, as well as with the staff involved with major gift solicitations.

The close of the general policy should include the caveat that the president or executive director of the nonprofit organization has final approval for naming interior properties, and that the board of governors, regents, or trustees has final approval (on recommendation from the president) to name buildings and outdoor spaces.

Buildings and Outdoor Properties. The construction of new buildings has attracted the largest share of named gifts in the last five years. Enamored with the notion of leaving their legacy gift for a shiny new building, donors appear to prefer the concept of supporting something new rather than giving a naming gift for an existing structure. Gifts in the range of $50 million are becoming commonplace.

The ask amount to name a building was the starting point for most lists of naming opportunities until recently. Naming gifts to schools of business are taking a backseat to gifts to schools of medicine, engineering, nursing, or public health. Deciding which buildings or facilities are available for the current campaign is also taking on greater strategic importance.

Universities and colleges with expansive campus grounds have been leveraging this trend by replacing aging facilities and adding new ones. The new construction phenomenon has become integral, where the billion dollar campaigns get their launch coordinates. Market activity suggests that developing a list of naming opportunities centered on a primary building remains a popular approach.

Determining which properties to list among the current naming opportunities is a little more complicated than it was two years ago. It's a hot marketplace for naming rights to high-profile properties. Two or three years from now, will there still be the same amount of interest? The crystal ball on my desk says yes, because the law of scarcity and the law of demand will most likely continue to force prices upward.

The general rule of thumb for naming a newly constructed building or outdoor space is a donation equivalent to 50% of the project cost. Depending on the nonprofit organization, this may or may not include an amount for an operating endowment. New construction projects are best handled on a case-by-case basis with regards to budget, project costs, and related naming opportunities.

Included with the 50% ask amount to name a building or outdoor space is the stipulation that the gift should be realized within a stated period of time. Five years is used as the maximum time limit in most naming situations.

This area of the naming rights policy should also spell out the wording for the naming of a building for an individual or family gift.

Last but not least, this section should include an outline of the context of the duration of naming rights for the building or outdoor area. Typical wording includes:

> The name will remain on the building or outdoor area for the life of the building or outdoor area. If at some time in the future the building or area is replaced, which may include a major reconstruction, the name may or may not be carried on the replacement facility as approved by the Board of Regents. If the name is not used on the replacement facility, the Board of Regents will determine the appropriate recognition to be incorporated into the new building.
>
> From the University of Washington Facilities and Naming Policy, reprinted with the university's consent. (See the Appendix for the complete document.)

An emerging naming rights trend is the inclusion of ask amounts for existing buildings. Few nonprofit groups outside higher education have the capacity or the option to construct new facilities. They work with what they have. This means trying to sell the naming rights for existing buildings, outdoor spaces, and other exterior naming opportunities.

During the past three years, I have come across several examples of nonprofit groups developing naming policies specifically for existing buildings and related properties. As compared to new construction projects, existing buildings create a unique dilemma for development staff. Rather than asking how much the ask amount should be, it might be better ask what the building is worth in the eyes of a prospective donor.

Some groups have looked back to the historical cost of the building to determine the ask amount to name the property. If the property is more than a few years old, however, that theory does not seem valid, because the property was built with money from a different time in the history of the organization.

A few organizations suggest that the nonprofit should stick to generally accepted accounting principles and use historical costs as the base point for determining the current ask amount to name the building. I wonder about that notion. What's the correlation between the cost of construction on a project done 10, 15, or 20 years ago and the current market conditions for naming rights? If we were to follow that line of thinking, we would determine the sale price for our homes based on what it cost to build them years ago. Any takers? Not likely.

The marketplace for naming rights on existing structures is influenced by many factors, not least of which is scarcity of a similar naming opportunity. Developing a benchmark of comparable properties is a much more effective way to establish an appropriate ask amount for a property.

While you are thinking about that, here is a significant new trend to consider: naming an entire campus. This trend appears to have grown out of the billion-dollar campaigns that have sprung up in and out of higher education. For discussion purposes, I am including naming a campus in the category of outdoor spaces, because they are expansive in coverage and not limited to a single building. Here are two recent examples:

1. September 12, 2007—Baylor University School of Medicine named the McNair Campus in appreciation of a $100 million gift from the Robert and Janice McNair Foundation.

   It is interesting to note that two years earlier, Dan Duncan (who is also a trustee of Baylor) gave the university a $100 million gift. In turn, the university named the Duncan Cancer Center for his gift. After a while, even the big universities will run out of properties to name, but they will continue to attract these large gifts. Naming a campus after the donor is a bit of lateral thinking applied to what could be an awkward situation.

2. August 21, 2007—Gordon College in Massachusetts renamed its Wenham campus the Dale E. and Sarah Anne Fowler Campus after the couple made a $60 million gift to the school.

Gifts of this nature have a transformational effect. There's that term again. Look for it to appear with greater frequency in the years ahead.

One last note before moving on: In January 2008, the executive director of a regional hospital in suburban Toronto indicated that their upcoming campaign would feature a $150 million ask to name their new outdoor space. More comprehensive than a naming gift to a university campus, the naming rights to a hospital property include the residual benefit of a brand name for the source of the named gift. Development professionals may say the naming rights are secondary, but donors making these kinds of gifts think otherwise.

Exhibit 6.1 shows two examples of naming opportunities matrices for a health care and an arts type of organization. The template can easily be adapted to suit the majority of nonprofit organizations by changing the names along the leftmost column and across the top of the chart.

Interior Properties. Once your donors enter the building, the naming opportunities change dramatically. New construction or old, the areas and items that can be named are limited only by your imagination.

EXHIBIT 6.1 Health Care and Arts Naming Opportunities Matrix

Health Care

	Named Hospital	Named Research Endowments	Endowed Chairs	Named Interior Spaces
Children's Hospital				
General Hospital				
Cancer Treatment Center				
Cancer Research				
Medical Research Centers				

Arts and Culture

	Named Facility	Named Exhibit Sponsor	Named Performance Sponsor	Named Interior Spaces
Performing Arts				
Visual Arts				

Hospitals, for example, have taken on aggressive naming initiatives—but at what price? If you tell a prospective donor that there are more than 1,000 naming opportunities inside the hospital, they may become unsettled or even overwhelmed. Perhaps it is better to let donor recognition plaques and tribute pieces do the talking for you as you open a discussion about making a named gift for an interior space.

This section of the naming rights policy shares many of the same attributes as the former section for buildings and outdoor spaces in word and in style. Consistency in approach and content is one of your greatest assets when drawing up a naming rights policy. This applies to the time allowed for making the donation, as well as the term of the naming rights and the subjective rights of the president to decide on what's best. One subject that must be included, however, is that interior naming opportunities are not recognized on external building walls.

That leaves just one more subject, which is typically left vague in naming rights policy statements: how to come up with ask amounts for interior spaces, equipment, places, and other naming opportunities. For those who are curious to learn more, see the section titled "Research the Market, Create Benchmarks" in this chapter.

Endowment Gifts. The endowment gifts to a fundraising campaign come primarily from individuals who have a passion for the organization. Leadership gifts in particular that are solicited and made during the quiet phase of a campaign, can help to set the tone and build momentum for other named gifts. At the public launch of the campaign, it is important to scroll back in time to the naming gifts made to help get the campaign to this stage.

In most campaigns, the majority of fundraising gifts come from individuals. Include a section in your naming rights policy just for this group.

Nonprofits have a wide assortment of naming opportunities, and the naming policies may be slightly different depending on what type of property is to be named. Grouping similar properties helps to define the boundaries; for example, buildings and outdoor areas are treated differently from indoor naming opportunities.

Naming rights for a building or other outdoor space do not generally extend to name recognition on the indoors of the building.

This section of the naming rights policy should also include the qualifying criteria for a named gift. The criteria may include the nature of the donor's relationship with the organization and the gift amounts appropriate to name designated properties. With buildings and outdoor spaces, a wide range of giving scenarios must be considered, including the dollar amounts appropriate for each.

Corporate and Organization Naming Rights. As the campaign moves along you may have corporate supporters that want to get involved. Including a naming rights policy provision for this type of charitable support is important for both parties.

The nonprofit sector has begun to see a tidal wave of corporate acquisitions of nonprofit naming rights on a multitude of properties. Having a policy in place to work with corporate partners is becoming increasingly important.

When you refer to the corporate naming policies in the Appendix, you will find that they use wording that is very similar in style and content to that for individuals. Whether the naming opportunities are for buildings, outdoor spaces, or interior spaces, it is important to develop a naming rights policy that offers a consistent framework for discussions between different types of funding sources. The unique attributes of a corporate gift are left to the naming rights agreement document, which is signed by both parties.

Approval of Naming Rights Gifts. The approval of the naming rights gift is another key area of the naming rights policy statement. Some organizations go so far as to list precisely which members of the development staff and administration will form the naming rights committee that handles the approval process.

Development staff, board members, and key volunteers should know about and understand how the naming rights approval process works. Whether you have a large organization or a small nonprofit group, you must have a documented approval process for all interested parties. Shortcuts in the approval process can lead to big problems later.

Nonprofit best practices for approval include the establishment and use of a naming rights committee, with layers of subcommittees based on the size and geographic location of members of the organization. It is critically important to establish a naming rights approval hierarchy that is well defined in terms of members, responsibilities, and authority.

For example, at many universities it is customary that the chancellor or president of the university is a member of the naming rights committee. By using a committee instead of leaving the total responsibility for naming rights decisions on the shoulders of one person, it narrows the gap for making a decision that may be difficult to undo later on.

The naming rights committee could be made up of members from the board of governors, the senior development staff person, the executive director, or president of the nonprofit organization with non-voting members, which may include the director of research and director of alumni affairs. It is especially important that other members of the nonprofit organization know of and understand the responsibility and authority for naming rights matters.

The policy should indicate that the president has final approval for the naming rights to interior spaces and the board of governors, regents, or trustees has authority (with recommendations from the president) over naming rights to outdoor buildings, outdoor spaces and indoor properties.

Recognition. The final component of a naming rights policy should cover recognition of the named property. One example that circulates in the health-care community is that the nonprofit entity should set aside 1% of the dollar value of the named gift (up to a maximum of a stated dollar amount) for recognition and stewardship activities.

Using a pre-established percentage of the gift helps to bring certainty to the recognition part of the process. Other nonprofits have a variety of financial formulas and dollar amount maximums in place to direct donor recognition activities. Developing a standardized dollar amount or percentage rate of the named gift is a recommended starting point. As always, there will be exceptions to the rules.

INSTITUTIONALIZE NAMING RIGHTS POLICIES

The ability to speak as if with one voice is what I mean by institutionalizing an administrative policy. How effectively a nonprofit organization can institutionalize their naming rights policy is a measure of leadership style and the culture of teamwork within the organization.

In 2001, I listened to a speech given by President Semple of University of Southern California during an the AFP Los Angles luncheon. That speech was my introduction to what it means to institutionalize a policy, how the policy permeates the culture of the organization. On that afternoon, the leader of one of America's top universities shared his behind-the-scenes perspectives on the university's recent success in their billion-dollar campaign, one of the first ever. As the packed house in the ballroom of the Pasadena Convention Center leaned forward to catch every word of his talk, President Semple was able to condense the magic of this marvelous accomplishment into two words: *compelling excellence.*

That was, he said, the mantra for everyone on the development team at USC. That was the message they shared with the donor community. Those two words became a focal point for everyone on the development team. They spoke about compelling excellence in every conversation with prospective donors. They talked about the best students, the best professors, the best programs, and USC's goal of achieving compelling excellence for the future. They were able to speak to prospective donors as if with one voice. The results were astounding: USC's campaign was one of the first nonprofit fundraising campaigns to break the $1 billion mark.

Getting It Done

Your organization's leadership must institutionalize the naming rights policy and support the efforts of the major gift officers, planned giving, annual giving, donor relations, and stewardship staff who represent the nonprofit organization to the donor community.

This unification of theme is a big challenge facing nonprofits. Being able to communicate not only the technical terms of the naming rights policy but also the consistent application takes a serious commitment, especially in a sector that is notorious for a high rate of employee turnover.

Developing the policy typically falls on the shoulders of the fundraising leadership of the organization. Implementing and institutionalizing the policy has become the responsibility of the donor relations and stewardship office.

Research the Market, Create Benchmarks

In order to come up with the appropriate dollar amounts for your naming opportunities you should take the time to research the marketplace. The use of benchmarks has become entrenched as a management technique, with various applications in the day-to-day operations of a nonprofit organization. For the purposes of this discussion, I define benchmarking as a process designed to facilitate information gathering, analysis, and decision making based on current market activity. Benchmarking is designed to put the decision makers in an informed position before they make policy and other leadership decisions.

Three Steps to Develop a Benchmark Report. An effective benchmark report pulls together data from a wide variety of sources and organizes it for analysis. Over the last 10 years, I have worked on benchmark reports for clients in the nonprofit and private sectors. Here is the three-step process I like to use when taking on one of these research projects.

Step 1. Conduct an in-depth survey based on information from the leadership of the organization. Start with a list of peer organizations and expand the information-gathering net outward from there.

Step 2. Standardize the information-gathering process by using templates to gather the data.

Step 3. Cast a wide net to include recent and current nonprofit and private sector lists of naming opportunities and completed naming rights deals.

For the benchmark report to have the greatest impact, the research-gathering process should include information from the following:

- Lists of current naming opportunities from peer groups and other local and regional nonprofits that are in campaign.
- News clippings and press releases about recent naming rights gifts, including dollar amounts and the name of the funding organization.
- Recent data on private sector naming rights deals such as multi-use centers, arts and culture venues, health-care facilities, amateur and professional sports facilities.

Collecting the data systematically and presenting it in an organized style will likely give the best results. Using a research team that understands the nature of the upcoming campaign and the kind of naming opportunities that will be included will help guide the information-gathering process for the research staff.

To offer the best value possible, the benchmark report must include data about nonprofits outside the direct circle of competitors. By that I mean that if the benchmark report is for a hospital, the data gathering must include information from the education sector, the arts and culture sector, the United Way, and local professional sports organizations. Leaving out any corner of the naming rights marketplace will compromise the overall quality of the information and the subsequent naming rights decisions that will come from it.

Exhibit 6.2 offers a benchmark template that can be used during the information-gathering process. By customers the list on the left side to your needs, you can specify which peer groups to include for your own benchmarking.

The asking price for the highest-profile naming opportunity will help to define how wide a net to cast during the information-gathering process. The larger the ask amount, the wider the net.

NAMING RIGHTS AGREEMENT

Another important document in the naming rights process is the actual naming rights agreement, which is signed by both parties. Best practices suggest that the major gifts or senior development officer who arranged for the named gift should "hand off" to the donor relations department to finalize the arrangements.

EXHIBIT 6.2 Benchmark Template

Higher Education

	Named Schools	Endowed Chairs	Named Centers	Athletics
National Universities and Colleges				
Tier-Two to Tier-Four Universities and Colleges				
Community Colleges				
Private Schools				
High Schools				
School Districts				
Hospitals and Health Care				
Arts Organizations				
United Way Sponsors				
Private Sector Sponsors				

When the gift is from an individual, the donor relations staff will arrange for a face-to-face meeting with the person (or with the executor of the will, in the case of an estate gift). The naming rights agreement will set out the details of the gift, including dollar amount, payment terms, and donor recognition details.

It has become more common for individuals who have committed to making substantial financial gifts to want to be actively involved in an ongoing manner. This expectation has grown in relation to the dollar amounts, because the donors see their gifts as investments in the nonprofit's future endeavors. People expect a higher level of accountability and disclosure before and after making their gifts. Donor relations staff has had to and will most likely continue to make adjustments to standardized naming rights agreements in order to meet donors' requests.

Limitations of space in this chapter do not allow for the reproduction of naming rights agreements. An online search will produce a plethora of hyperlinks to a wide variety of documents that will satisfy your curiosity.

Review and/or Develop Web Site Strategy

Having a naming rights strategy that includes the nonprofit's Web site is critical in today's online world. When more than 20% of the world's population has access to the Internet, as noted by World Internet Stats in January of 2008, and the annual rate of growth of internet users is at 17%, nonprofits need to get in the game of online communication.

By now it is quite likely that your organization has invested heavily in its Web site. I suggest to you that this commodity is more than just a digital billboard that occasionally catches the eye of a passerby. Your Web site is a vibrant portal to the people on the World Wide Web who are constantly looking for interesting stories, eager to find out about what's going on, and looking to share stuff with their friends.

Do you have a Web page right now for online giving? Can someone that visits your Web site in the next 30 seconds go to a dedicated Web page and make a charitable contribution to your organization? A growing number of nonprofits can offer that today.

If your organization is doing that, what are you doing for those people who are interested in your capital campaign? If the answer is nothing, I suggest that you are missing out on opportunities to engage your donor and prospective donors. What if just one person learned about your fundraising campaign and the naming opportunities currently available by visiting your Web site? That person contacts your organization and it leads to a major gift. What is that worth to the organization? Viewed another way, what is it costing you by not being there?

Recommendations for Developing a Web Site Strategy. A nonprofit that has an online giving program usually follows that with a Planned Giving Web page on their site. The next step is to talk about the campaign and the naming opportunities where donors can get involved and support what you do. Here are some suggestions for developing your Web site strategy:

1. Create a dedicated section of the Web site that integrates the campaign and naming opportunities.

2. Include a section on donor gifts already received. Use a photo of the donor(s) and include a press release if there was a naming gift announcement.

3. Start with a simple message. You can use either the shopping list approach to itemize the properties available to be named and their respective ask amounts or you could use the descriptive text approach. See the examples shown in the table below:

Approaches for Naming Opportunities

Shopping List Approach

Name the building	$5,000,000
Lobby	$1,000,000
Auditorium	$750,000
Conference room	$500,000
Small meeting room	$125,000
Executive office suite	$100,000
Administrative office	$50,000

Descriptive Text Approach

Project Leader Medical Research
Endowing a Project Leader Medical research helps our organization to recruit, retain, and reward its best and

brightest medical research staff. With a gift of $1.25 million, you can establish a permanent fund to underwrite the medical research efforts of a project leader for one of our teams, allowing him or her to seek out innovative approaches to cancer care and treatments.

As with other elements in the Manager's Toolbox, I recommend you keep it simple and add a layer to your Web site one section at a time. A consistent message over the long term will help to bolster the communication with your donor community.

Demographics

How well do you know the demographics of your community? Can you share that information in a one page summary? When you can do that you have leverage that you can use in your discussions with funding sources.

Any group that you send a grant proposal to will want to know about your constituency. Who is involved? How many families or individuals do you serve? What kind of services do you provide? How often? Where are these offered? Demographic data that offers big picture and small group details will help to prove your case for support.

Corporations in particular are often looking for ways to link up with new market opportunities. Getting the brand name out in front of the consumer matters most to a corporation when there is a "good fit" between the demographics of their consumer and your own. Whether you are looking for a performance sponsor for an upcoming production, or you want to find a title sponsor for a black tie event, or maybe some corporate support for an annual golf tournament, demographic details help to tell your story.

And by the way, consider posting some of this demographic information on your Web site along with the naming opportunities. Funding organizations who will be visiting your Web site can connect the dots for themselves when they have more details to do an in-depth evaluation of your proposal.

Pricing Strategies

The pricing strategies you choose will have a direct impact on the ask amounts of the naming opportunities. Define the style of naming rights the organization is prepared to offer. Will the rights be offered in perpetuity or for a limited number of years? This is a critical decision in the planning process, and there are pros and cons to both options.

Let's take a few minutes to examine both. The long-standing tradition is to use "in perpetuity" as the basis for the named gift. By choosing this strategy the donor and the nonprofit organization is certain about the nature of his/her gift in terms of the time frame that it will be recognized within. With the turnover of properties and redevelopment of facilities every twenty, thirty, or forty years, it is generally accepted that the naming legacy or naming recognition will be limited to the life of the property. In some cases, the buildings or spaces last longer and the naming gift stays with the property throughout its lifetime.

If the named gift was for an endowment in perpetuity then there are no restrictions on the length of term. As in the example of the endowed chairs set up at Oxford and Harvard hundreds of years ago, they both still exist today.

The advantages of using the "in perpetuity" strategy include the notion of fitting in with the status quo and of the gift being of similar style to those of the majority of other donors. Many people like the idea of a legacy gift that will continue to benefit the nonprofit long after they have died. It fits in with some of the cultural and ethnic traditions of charitable support that began generations before and is something continued on today.

The altruistic nature of a nonprofit organization is bigger than the lifetime of one person and the gift made in perpetuity has evolved as a meaningful way for an individual or group to add to the financial security in the years ahead. A negative impact of using "in perpetuity" for naming opportunities is that the dollar amount to make such a gift is quite often outside the financial reach of many donors. Another is that this strategy limits the number of giving opportunities as compared to a "limited term" naming strategy.

The "limited term" naming strategy is just as the label implies. The donor makes a gift to support the nonprofit and the length of the term is preestablished at the time the gift is made.

A limited term strategy is common in the private sector where corporations that are looking for ways to boost their own brand name have been buying naming rights to facilities such as stadiums, arenas, multifunction facilities, and conference centers.

In recent years, a growing number of nonprofits have borrowed from that strategy to develop a "limited term" naming strategy for their own giving opportunities. In the arts and culture sector in particular, we find many examples of this strategy being used.

In my discussions with Gene Gregory, Vice President of Development at the Oregon Symphony Orchestra, he indicated that using the limited term naming strategy enabled him to have many more discussions with prospective donors about getting involved in supporting the orchestra. In this case, the Oregon Symphony Orchestra gave people four choices to support a particular area of interest. Those choices ranged from a named gift "in perpetuity" to three limited terms of ten years, five years, and three years.

In the following table, you can see the built-in flexibility a "limited term" strategy offers a campaign. The number of giving opportunities increases from seven to 28, four times the number. Perhaps the most significant aspect is the expanded dollar range now available to prospective supporters.

Example of a Limited Term Exhibit: Naming Opportunities Campaign

Endowed Chair or Endowed Program	Endow in Perpetuity	Name for 10 Years	Name for Five Years	Name for Three Years
Principal Chair	$1,500,000	$750,000	$375,000	$225,000
Assistant Principal Chair	$1,250,000	$625,000	$312,500	$187,500
Section Chair	$1,000,000	$500,000	$250,000	$150,000
Classical Applause Series	$10,000,000	$5,000,000	$2,500,000	$1,500,000
Classical Bravo Series	$10,000,000	$5,000,000	$2,500,000	$1,500,000
Pops Series	$6,000,000	$3,000,000	$1,500,000	$900,000
Symphony Sundays	$5,000,000	$2,500,000	$1,250,000	$750,000

A limited term strategy can be blended in with "in perpetuity" as shown in the table above, or left standing on it's own. If you leave out the "in perpetuity" option, then you are more than likely to limit the perception of the donor who has the capacity and interest to make a much larger gift.

The pricing hierarchy for limited term gifts takes its lead from the ask amount to name a property in perpetuity. In over 90% of the pricing strategies I have examined, nonprofits typically use a double-up and/or double-down when setting the ask amounts for named gifts.

If the ask amount to name an endowment is $10 million and the second choice is to name the same endowment for a 10-year period, the pricing strategy used most often would be to use an ask amount that is 50% of the amount to name the gift in perpetuity. When using the "limited term" approach, that same pricing formula often extends to other limited term ask amounts except for the last choice. At this level, the majority of nonprofits use a fixed minimum dollar amount that is often outside the double-up formula in part because they would like to encourage the larger gift and, in part, to set a minimum standard for making a named gift.

The table on the previous page is just one example of a limited term strategy. Other strategies could easily expand or contract the range of choices for donors to consider. Perhaps the most significant aspect is that this strategy is gaining widespread acceptance in nonprofits outside the higher education and health care sector—the two areas that continue to attract the largest number of donors and the most money in their fundraising campaigns.

Hierarchy of Naming Rights in the Pricing Strategy. The pricing strategies for selling naming rights used by nonprofits have yet to show much creativity. In less than 2% of the 30,000 naming opportunities in my survey did I find dollar values for the ask amounts that were something other than the typical double-up and double-down price structure. Check out the example in the following table:

Double-Up and Double-Down Price Structure

Ask Amounts for Naming Rights Using the Double Up/Double-Down Technique

Name the Building	$10 million
Name the Lobby	$5 million
Name the Conference Center	$2.5 million
Name the Library	$1 million
Name the Atrium	$500,000
Name the Board Room	$250,000
Name the Large Classroom	$100,000
Name the Small Classroom	$50,000
Name the President's Office	$20,000
Name other offices, each	$10,000

Look familiar? You are absolutely correct. The hypothetical list above is not perfectly symmetrical in descending order of dollar values, but you get the picture. The vast majority of nonprofit organizations use the double-up/double-down pricing approach to attach dollar values to their naming opportunities. The tactic is not limited to physical properties but is applied to endowment giving opportunities as well:

Name a President's Endowed Chair	$5 million
Name a Dean's Endowed Chair	$2.5 million
Name a Graduate Scholarship Fund	$2 million
Name an Undergraduate Scholarship Fund	$1 million
Name a Partial Scholarship Fund	$500,000

Those who take the time to do benchmark information gathering will find numerous examples of this pricing model in place at peer organizations. In a competitive market situation, do you want to be just like everyone else? What will your pricing strategy for naming opportunities reveal to prospective donors? More of the same or something unique? Food for thought.

Celebrate Leadership Named Gifts

Take the time to celebrate every one of the leadership gifts that came in during the quiet phase of the campaign. They represent much more than a large check going into the organization's bank account. Donors who made the decision to step up and give leadership level financial support take on a legacy status that cannot be valued with a conventional measuring stick.

A celebration at the naming ceremony is just the start of how an organization can celebrate leadership gifts. Permanent recognition in the form of a named facility or property extends forward in time. Nonprofits that combine the physical name recognition along with a virtual acknowledgement on their Web site get the best of both worlds.

Web sites are used to tell the story about an organization. Why not set aside a few Web pages to say thank you to your leadership gift supporters? A digital archive is easy to set up and takes little maintenance once it has been established. This could be considered the next layer in advanced donor relations. Take a moment to think about it.

Sharing Naming Rights Information with the Donor Community. Senior development staff do not appear to be in agreement on the best way to tackle this part of the naming rights game. Should they or should they not make public their list of naming opportunities? A growing number of nonprofits are choosing to share that information via hard copy reports, periodic newsletters, or specially designed campaign promotional material.

Every week, more nonprofit organizations are taking things a step farther by adding the list of their naming opportunities to their Web sites. In the winter of 2008, it was estimated that there were more than 50,000 naming opportunities published on the Web sites of nonprofits.

Approximately 20% of the global population, more than 1.3 billion people, use the Internet. The nonprofits that have gone the extra mile are gaining a competitive advantage, because their information is available online 24/7.

STEWARDSHIP

Engaging the donor in stewardship activities begins the moment after they have said yes. Once someone has made the first step toward a major gift to the nonprofit organization, it is important that the development staff change gears in the conversation and put on the stewardship hat for the rest of the conversation.

If you don't already have staff dedicated to stewardship responsibilities, you might want to consider adding those positions to your organization. Stewardship is a thoughtful and engaging process designed to build on the existing relationship with the donor and enable it to move to another level. Major gifts that result in naming rights receive varying amounts and types of stewardship-related communication based on the dollar value of the gift, from thank-you letters signed by development staff right up to personal notes, telephone calls, and in-person greetings from the executive director or president of the nonprofit organization. Stewardship is now recognized as one of the most important functions, one that will facilitate a meaningful ongoing relationship with the donor.

Going Another Mile

Stewardship best practices have continued to evolve. The most notable shift is toward developing stewardship action plans for top donors. Two years ago, I interviewed the donor relations staff at Hamilton College, a liberal arts private school in upstate New York. At the time, the staff had just begun to implement stewardship action plans with their top 10 donors. The thinking was that the college already had invested a lot of time in the relationships that had come as a result of their top donors' ongoing support of the college. The donor relations team felt that it was time to become more active in the stewardship process—in effect, to learn more about these people, including the things they were most passionate about. The team developed customized stewardship plans for each individual on the top 10 list, and planned to extend that process to the top 25 donors over the next year.

The stewardship effort has paid off nicely for Hamilton College. The current fundraising campaign that grew from the action plans for major donors has lead to a surge in major gifts, many recognized with appropriate naming rights. The most prominent to date has been the $10-million gift from one couple to establish a three-building arts complex. As of mid-February 2008, other named gifts to Hamilton College include named endowed professorships, a named admissions office, a named theater, and the establishment of a wireless computer network on campus. Stewardship action plans appear to have paid off.

Trends show that once a donor makes an initial major gift, the probability that they will make another, perhaps of greater value in the future, rises dramatically. The style of communication between the donor and the nonprofit between those two major gifts is part of the moves management strategy employed today. Stewardship is the key, and named gifts may be one of the benefits of a lasting relationship.

~ 7 ~

Corporate Naming Rights with Strings Attached

Nonprofit organizations must expect that when they are selling their naming rights to a corporate sponsor, the agreement comes with strings attached. An important point to raise early in this chapter is that the wording of the naming rights agreement is such that the nonprofit has wiggle room if needed sometime in the future to dissolve the agreement and remove the corporate name from the property. With corporate scandals like the embezzlement by Enron key executives or massive overstating of revenue at WorldCom in the rearview mirror, nonprofits need to have the option to dissolve the naming rights agreement at the discretion of the board of directors. In the Appendix of this book you will find naming rights agreements from both the University of Pittsburgh and the University of Washington that includes this type of wording. Donors put their trust and their financial resources in the hands of nonprofits and expect a high level of accountability and discretion when it comes to important decisions such as which corporations can align themselves with a nonprofit entity. Whether it is the naming rights agreement for $25 million at the University of Texas, Austin to name the AT&T Executive Education & Conference Center, or the $1-million gift from the local furniture store to name the performing arts venue, naming rights come with certain expectations on deliverables.

The more comprehensive the package of deliverables a nonprofit organization can bundle together, the better its negotiating position will be. Corporations make decisions based on building their brand names and enhancing their positions in the marketplace. Understanding their goals, the demographics of their market, and that the ways that these match your own community is the basis for the discussions about corporate sponsorship.

Let's work through an example. A corporate sponsor is interested in the outdoor naming rights to an existing building—a stadium, performing arts venue, or multi-event facility. In the following section, you will find lists of communication and marketing perks to offer your potential corporate sponsor/partner. Once you open the door to offer naming rights, you are inviting in corporate strangers. You need to get to know them, and they need to get to know you.

BENEFITS OF CORPORATE SPONSORSHIP

Here are some of the tangible and intangible benefits that a nonprofit may include in a naming rights discussion:

Communication benefits may include:

- Pre-event naming ceremony
- Media invited to cover naming ceremony
- Outdoor signage for the term of contract
- Naming rights extended to print material
- Web site recognition where appropriate

Marketing opportunities may include:

- On-site promotional kiosks
- Extent of interior name recognition signage
- Company staff on-site during special events
- Ability to conduct on-site product demonstrations
- Ability to conduct on-site surveys
- Day-of-the-event marketing presence
- Tickets to the event for customers
- Private suite access
- Corporate name in promotional literature

- Extend special offers by corporate partner to the Web site

Perceived value for naming rights is a two-way mirror. It's a part of business. Be aware that the company handing over the big check has a perceived value of the naming rights that is greater than the asking price. That is a good thing. I'm not suggesting that you need to go out and change the ask amounts, especially for the high-profile properties.

When perceived value over the length of the naming rights contract is greater than the asking price it's a good business decision to evaluate further to see if it makes sense for the corporation to get involved. Philanthropy is a small part of the corporate decision to become a naming rights sponsor. If you think in terms of percentage points of market share for the corporation, you begin to see the opportunity from their point of view.

GETTING TO YES WITH A CORPORATE PARTNER

On the nonprofit side of the ledger, the ask amount was developed using some type of benchmarking process and was deemed to be fair given the current market conditions.

On the corporate side of the ledger, the dollars paid for naming rights are perceived as an investment in property that allows for marketing and promotional activities related to the company's products and services. Invariably, there will be a

sponsorship checklist of direct and indirect benefits that the corporation wants before signing the
deal and handing over the check. Ask for their
list early in the discussion. Be prepared to share
in-depth marketing-style data with your corporate
counterparts.

As discussions move forward with a prospective
corporate sponsor, there are a few things you can do:

- Provide an overview of the organization.
- Invite the marketing staff to visit the facilities.
- Conduct a hard-hat tour for new construction
  sites.
- Ask questions about their products and services.
- Look for common ground.
- Be prepared to break from the status quo.
- Think in terms of having a financial partner
  involved with the organization.

Managing expectations on both sides of a naming rights deal are tremendously important to form-
ing a solid foundation for a long-term relationship.

THREE TIERS OF CORPORATE NAMING RIGHTS

As we examine the naming rights marketplace in
early 2008, we can split it into three groups.

1. *King Midas Naming Rights*—This group
   includes the upper echelon of naming rights

deals in both the private sector and the non-profit. With playful reference to the mythical king that could turn things into gold, there are some naming rights deals, such as the $400 million deals made by Citi Bank and Barclays Bank to name professional sports stadiums in New York, that have set the bar incredibly high for others.

2. *Golden Egg Naming Rights*—Think billion-dollar fundraising campaigns, in which the ask amounts to name a property start at $10 million and go up to $200 million or more. Announcements for what I refer to as the Golden Egg type of naming rights arrive almost weekly these days. Having a major gift strategy that focuses on large gifts from major donors is the key to attracting these type of legacy gifts.

3. *Lasting Legacy Naming Rights*—Stewardship activities and effort on donor relations that enhance long-term relationships will result in lasting legacy naming rights gifts. Competition for major gifts is likely to intensify, and donors have plenty of choices. Committed stewardship will win the day.

MANAGING THE NAMING RIGHTS PROPERTIES

Earlier in the book, I mentioned an example of the growing international influence in the naming rights marketplace: the naming of the Barclays

Center in Brooklyn. The $400-million naming rights deal equates to $20 million per year from a British-owned bank. It's very interesting to note that a U.S. company was not the winning bidder on that property, especially in New York City. In the same breath, think about how the international business community looks at naming rights properties in the United States as compared to other countries around the world.

Barclays Bank is one of the global leaders in international wealth management. It is no coincidence that Barclays chose New York, home of the New York Stock Exchange and the epicenter of the American financial community, as the place to buy a named property.

The company looks at named properties as acquiring a strategic investment. Managing the investment in those properties requires a long-term plan that integrates multiple levels of the local and international sales and marketing effort.

Barclays Center, Brooklyn	$400 million 2007 20 year naming rights
Barclays English Premiership	Title Sponsor
£ 65.8 million for 3 years	2007–2010
£ 57 million for 3 years	2004–2006
Australian Rugby	Broadcast Sponsor 2007

Barclays president Bob Diamond said of the company's sponsorship deal for the Barclays English Premiership soccer league that it fit the firm's expanding international business agenda.

When we look at naming rights from a broader perspective, we can begin to understand the strategic importance of top-tier American properties. The international appeal comes from the leverage gained in boosting brand name in the U.S. market.

A New York Naming Bonanza

Across town, the Citi Bank deal was for an equal $400 million to name the new baseball stadium for the New York Mets. Other naming opportunities exist throughout the nonprofit sector of America's largest city. From the local universities and colleges to hospitals, research facilities, and a long list of other groups, named properties are available for sale. How long will it be before we see more corporate acquisitions in the nonprofit sector as compared to the private sector in New York?

Exhibit 7.1 compares three naming rights deals in the New York area to a recent agreement signed in Cleveland, Ohio. The baseball stadium in Cleveland was renamed Progressive Field in late 2007, when Progressive, an insurance company that was founded in Cleveland, signed a 16-year naming agreement. Here is a case of local company that made it big and can be seen to be giving back to

EXHIBIT 7.1 Naming Rights Deals: New York City and Cleveland, Ohio

Arena	Barclays Center Brooklyn, NY	Citi Field New York, NY	IZOD Center Meadowlands, New Jersey	Progressive Field Cleveland, OH
Dollar Amount	$400 million	$400 million	$10 million	$57.6 million
Term for Naming Rights	20 years	20 years	5 years	16 years
Team Association	Multi-event facility; NBA: New Jersey Nets (open 2009–2010 season)	Major League Baseball: New York Mets	Multi-event facility; NBA: New Jersey Nets (for 2007–2009 season)	Major League Baseball: Cleveland Indians
Sponsor Type	International financial services	U.S.-based financial services	Retail clothing	Insurance company
Population Base	20 million	20 million	20 million	2.2 million

the community by supporting the local baseball club and picking up the naming rights to the stadium. In the competitive business of baseball the amount of money that comes from annual naming rights fees may be the difference in signing that one key player who could make a difference to a championship team. The dollar value of the naming rights agreement signed by Progressive Insurance is estimated to be worth approximately $3.6 million per year.

In New Jersey, the Meadowlands Sports Authority had a dilemma on its hands. The naming rights to the Sports Authority's aging multi-event facility, formerly called the Continental Airlines Arena, had just expired. What to do?

They put it up for bid. Phillips-Van Heusen Corporation's IZOD brand outbid other midsize firms, including Racewear and Southpole, both of which are also members of the New York fashion and clothing industry. IZOD won with an offer of $2 million per year for a 5-year term. Compared to the other New York area naming rights deals, this pales in comparison. But there were not a lot of bidders in the running.

Long-term prospects for the property will be tied to the Xanadu retail-entertainment complex that is currently under construction, rather than to the center's historical link to pro sports teams. The NBA's New Jersey Nets will play the next two seasons in the IZOD Center and then relocate to the new Barclays Center for the 2009 season. The NHL's New Jersey Devils already vacated the premises at the start of the 2007 season.

MARKETPLACE DEFINES DOLLAR VALUES

Dollar values for naming rights are driven by several key factors:

- Pro sports team as a primary tenant
- Multi-event facilities offer marketing diversity
- Media coverage

In the private sector, it starts with a professional sports team being a primary tenant. Baseball attracts a massive amount of corporate dollars, due in large part to the length of the season, the number of games played, and the traditions that accompany postseason playoffs.

Multi-event venues like the Barclays in New York and others across the country provide more diverse brand-name exposure and marketing opportunities compared to facilities with a single function, such as baseball.

In the coming months of 2008, we will most likely see two or perhaps three other corporate naming rights deals for professional sports venues: one in Washington, D.C., one in San Francisco, and possibly one in Tennessee.

LENGTH OF TERM DEPENDS ON THE PROPERTY

The corporate sector has fallen in love with the concept of acquiring naming rights. Naming rights deals in the private sector are typically offered on a *limited term naming rights agreement.* The length of the term for the naming rights varies considerably depending on the property involved. Marketing departments have to think in terms of brand name building, brand name enhancement and the relative impact on customer retention and customer loyalty.

As you review the list below keep in mind that this is a general reference to the types of naming rights properties that are being offered by nonprofit organizations. Some corporate partners find that the sponsorship or naming of an event really fits well with their market and may want to extend the length of term.

Before your organization commits to an extension be sure to get some feedback from both the sponsor and your own donor community to help make it a win-win for all parties. Here is a bird's-eye view of some of the current types of naming rights deals:

Title sponsorships:	1 to 5 years
Gala event sponsorship	1 to 3 years
Official supplier	3 to 5 years
Named pro sports building	10 to 20 years
Dollar value of naming rights	Shifting upwards
Choice of naming rights properties	Spreading across the nonprofit sector

BUNDLING THE NAMING RIGHTS FOR CORPORATE PARTNERS

The bundling of marketing opportunities is one of key areas that marketing staff review when evaluating potential naming opportunities. With the growing scarcity of high-profile properties in the private sector, we can expect to see an increasing number of corporate partners getting involved with nonprofit organizations.

To get a better understanding of this side of the marketplace, I spoke to Tom Stultz, Senior Vice President and Director of IMG College. The firm is one of America's leading collegiate marketing, licensing, and media companies.

IMG College works with a distinguished list of corporate clients that includes Alltel, Coca Cola, Gatorade, The National Milk Processor Board, IBM, New Balance, and State Farm Insurance. The company signed a $67-million athletics marketing deal with the University of Oregon in early February 2008—an agreement that will include negotiating the naming rights for the football stadium and a baseball park on the university's campus.

I asked Tom what he looks for when trying to match corporate clients with naming rights opportunities.

"We look for corporations that are compatible with our partner universities," said Stultz. He went on to talk about the method IMG College uses to qualify potential partners. Corporations that have a strong presence in the area or a natural affinity with the school make good potential partners for a naming rights agreement.

Stultz asked, "How do you make this a good investment?" He answered his own question: "It is the exposure of the name on the facility. There is an inventory that comes with naming rights, such as hospitality suites, tickets, and media exposure." He indicated that at IMG College they try to bundle it all together for their clients.

The corporation has to have some type of measurement to value the naming rights. Much of the analysis centers around the volume of media attention given to the property. According to Stultz, that ranges from eyeballs to media exposures over the life of the contract to how many people pass through the turnstiles. A naming rights package needs to be bundled so that it has a lot of value.

Naming rights in the nonprofit sector have taken on a new dimension. The corporate partners have already started to line up. Which ones will be next?

~ 8 ~

Where to Next for Naming Rights?

Where, indeed, will the paths for naming rights lead us next?

All signs indicate that the health-care sector will continue to attract more naming rights dollars. That includes both corporate sponsorships and legacy-style gifts to name children's hospitals, cancer clinics, pediatric centers, and medical research facilities. It won't stop there.

Endowment gifts to support designated staff positions will also continue to grow in number of endowed positions and in the relative dollar amount per endowment.

Academic institutions that already have multi-billion dollar endowment funds will continue to attract more and more named gifts. In most cases, the dollar values to name an endowment are already shifting upward and will likely to continue that trend for years to come. There are no limits when it comes to how much a donor will commit to in terms of making endowment gifts.

GROWTH POTENTIAL FOR NAMING RIGHTS

The marketplace for naming rights does not appear to have reached a saturation point as yet. In the years ahead, I believe we will see continued growth in the number and in the diversity of naming rights announcements.

The education sector continues to lead the way in terms of the number of naming opportunities currently available and the amounts that they are asking for. Universities and colleges, both public and private, as well as community colleges and private schools make up the largest percentage of naming rights on the market today.

Several niche markets for naming rights appear to be growing at double-digit rates, including the following:

- School districts, public schools, and religious schools
- Environmental groups for properties and programs
- Municipalities for a range of properties
- State and federal government properties, especially parks
- Medical research
- Arts and culture organizations

When we see funding organizations like the Walter and Flora Hewlett Foundation make a $113-million donation in September 2007 to the University of California, Berkeley, it's a sign that the upper limits of endowment gifts have shattered. Strategic in their giving, the foundation stipulated that $110 million must be matched by other donors to endow 100 faculty chairs across campus. Reports from Berkeley suggest that the development staff are a little busier these days.

For those who scoff at the notion of the significance of named endowment gifts relative to the dollar values for naming tangible properties, pause and think about your moves management strategy, if you have one. There is a direct correlation that can be drawn between endowment giving and subsequent named gifts at higher dollar amounts. The moves management strategy works when there is a generous helping of stewardship-related activity to engage and enrich the relationship with the donor.

On the other hand, the billion-dollar campaigns have turned a sharper focus towards attracting multi-million dollar major gifts, the kind that name a college, a hospital, or an entire campus. We are living in an era where the transfer of wealth from one generation to the next is unlike that of any other time in history. Funding sources have the capacity to give great amounts of cash. Naming rights that accrue to legacy donors or corporations will stand the test of time.

Appendix

This Appendix includes four documents for your review:

1. University of Pittsburgh Office of Institutional Advancement Named Facilities and Programs Policy
2. University of Washington: Facilities and Spaces Naming Policy (Campaign University of Washington: Creating Futures Facilities and Spaces Naming Policy)
3. Campaign University of Washington: Creating Futures Endowment and Program Naming Policy
4. Historic Named Gift Survey form

Each one of the policy statements is reprinted here with the express written permission of the issuing university.

UNIVERSITY OF PITTSBURGH OFFICE OF INSTITUTIONAL ADVANCEMENT NAMED FACILITIES AND PROGRAMS POLICY

Policy Owners: **Institutional Advancement (IA)**

Medical and Health Sciences Foundation (MHSF)

Department of Athletics

Office of the Executive Vice Chancellor

Office of General Counsel

Office of Finance

Facilities Management

Office of the Provost

Office of the Senior Vice Chancellor for the Health Sciences

TABLE OF CONTENTS

Drafted: 10/10/06
Revised: 7/17/07

1. POLICY STATEMENT

The named facilities and programs policy sets forth a framework for recommendations and the approval process for the naming of all University facilities or assets stewarded by the University and deposited into University accounts for Oakland, Bradford, Greensburg, Johnstown, and Titusville. This includes physical facilities, interior spaces, campus grounds, equipment, and programs to ensure that all naming opportunities are consistent and follow the interests of the University of Pittsburgh. All naming will be subject to periodic review to determine that the naming continues to be consistent with the interests of the University. For staff members who do not report to the Office of Institutional Advancement or the Medical and Health Sciences Foundation, contact one of the appropriate areas for assistance/consultation.

Policy Owners: Institutional Advancement (IA), University of Pittsburgh and University of Pittsburgh Medical Center and Health Sciences Foundation (MHSF), Department of Athletics, Office of the Executive Vice Chancellor, General Counsel, Office of Finance, Facilities Management, Office of Provost, Office of the Senior Vice Chancellor for the Health Sciences

2. POLICY PURPOSE

The purpose of the named facilities and programs policy is to provide clear and concise guidelines to University staff responsible for the solicitation of gifts for the naming of facilities and programs that are acceptable to the University following all legal and financial requirements.

All pre-existing approved named opportunities pricing lists will be grandfathered into this policy.

3. DEFINITION OF TERMS

Development Staff: Staff members from IA, MHSF and Athletics who are responsible for cultivation, solicitation and stewardship.

Capital Projects: Construction and/or renovation of capital facilities or equipment.

Capital Reserve Account: An account to hold surplus budget funds used for renovations, capital construction, or equipment purchase.

Current Fund: A fund which may be expended in its entirety by the University.

Endowment: A fund intended to provide support in perpetuity for a specific purpose designated by a donor. The principal is not expendable under the terms of the gift. The principal is invested with allocated income available and dedicated to supporting the stated purpose of the endowment.

Exceptions: Specific instances when a variation occurs from the standard outcome.

Facility: All buildings, additions to buildings, space in a building, outdoor spaces such as a garden, court or plaza, and other tangible and relatively permanent feature locations on any University property.

Drafted: 10/10/06
Revised: 7/17/07

Plant Fund: An account to hold funds for construction and/or renovations.

Procedures: Guidelines established to describe the method of operations for a specific task or function.

Production Standards: The minimum expected outcome of a given task or function to be implemented on a consistent basis.

4. RELATED DOCUMENTS

IA Website:
- Allocation Policy
- Gift Processing Policy
- University of Pittsburgh Gift Policy
- Planned Giving Policy
- Prospect Management Policy
- Stewardship Policy
- Agreement Policy
- Named Facilities/Programs Database (under construction)

5. CONTACTS

INSTITUTIONAL ADVANCEMENT (IA)

Subject	Contact	Telephone
Agreement Administration	Director, Advancement Operations (Agreement Administrator)	412-624-5829
Agreement Processing	Administrative Coordinator, Agreement and Quality Administration (Agreement Processor)	412-624-5846
Corporate/Foundation Relations	Associate Vice Chancellor, Central Giving Programs and Communications	412-624-5822
Gift/Pledge Processing	Director, Records Management	412-624-5855
Named Facilities Processing	Associate Vice Chancellor, Operations and Quality Administration	412-648-2168

Drafted: 10/10/06
Revised: 7/17/07

UNIVERSITY OF PITTSBURGH AND UNIVERSITY OF PITTSBURGH MEDICAL CENTER MEDICAL AND HEALTH SCIENCES FOUNDATION (MHSF)

Subject	Contact	Telephone
Agreement Administration	Director, Planned Giving (Agreement Administrator)	412-647-4220
Agreement Processing	Director of Operations (Agreement Processor)	412-647-4286
Named Facilities Processing	Director of Operations	412-647-4286

UNIVERSITY OF PITTSBURGH

Subject	Contact	Telephone
Agreement Interpretation (Legal)	Associate General Counsel	412-624-5993
Facilities Management	Associate Vice Chancellor	412-624-9510
Office of the Chancellor	Chancellor	412-624-4200
Office of the Executive Executive Vice Chancellor	Executive Vice Chancellor	412-624-4247
Office of the Provost	Provost	412-624-4223
Office of Senior Vice Chancellor for the Health Sciences	Senior Vice Chancellor, Health Sciences	412-648-8975
Office of the Secretary	Assistant Chancellor and Secretary	412-624-6623

6. NAMING REVIEW PROCESS

A. Purpose

The purpose of the Naming Review Process is to ensure that prior to approaching a prospect/donor to solicit a named opportunity for a facility or program that must be a permanent part of the University, the appropriate approvals are received by senior level administration.

B. Production Standards

- Approval on a case by case basis by the Dean/Director and Provost/Senior Vice Chancellor for the Health Sciences.

- Formulate the cost of the gift based on one or more of the following:

    - Type of space (conference room, office, laboratory, lecture hall, etc.)

    - Size of space

    - Cost of construction or renovation

    - Components within the space (equipment, furniture, fixtures, lighting, wall coverings, floor coverings, etc.)

Drafted: 10/10/06
Revised: 7/17/07

- Buildings must have approval by the Chancellor and Board of Trustees when appropriate following University Policy. Policy on Buildings

- Pre-approved minimum gift level amounts for facilities or programs must be approved by the appropriate senior level administrators before packaging, publishing and using for solicitation purposes. After two years, all prior approved items must be reevaluated.

- Although the Cathedral of Learning is a Campus Architectural Treasure, it will not be named. (Refer to *place link here for minimum pricing*)

C. Procedures
- Refer to Section 7.

7. NAMING REVIEW PROCEDURE

A. Purpose
The purpose of the Naming Review Procedure is to provide guidance to Development Staff on the process for the approval of named facilities and programs.

B. Production Standards
- Refer to Section 6.

C. Procedures
- Development staff member verifies that the facility or program is not already named.

- The gift is to be paid over a period of no longer than five (5) years.

- A space is named for a gift that is allocated for one of the following: (in no particular order)
    - A substantial endowment that is proportional to the amount necessary to sustain a school/program/research.

    - Total or partial cost of renovation and support of the facility.

    - A substantial endowment that is proportional to the amount necessary to sustain the facility.

    - Fifty percent of the gift supports the cost to renovate and sustain the facility and fifty percent is designated for research or programmatic support as deemed essential to the University.

    - Value assigned to a program is based on academic reputation of unit, annual operating budget, unit's per capita operating cost per student, and similar opportunity at peer institutions.

Drafted: 10/10/06
Revised: 7/17/07

- Development staff member prepares and submits the <u>Opportunity Request Form</u> to the Department of Operations and Quality Administration/ Director of Operations allowing up to 60 days for full completion of the process.

- Development staff member solicits prospect/donor once receiving final approval from the appropriate senior level administrator(s).

- Development staff member prepares agreement following the Agreement Policy.

- Design and renovation is conducted by Facilities Management.

8. NAMED FACILITIES RESOURCE

A. Purpose
The purpose of this section is to provide a comprehensive resource to staff of spaces within buildings such as, but not limited to, rooms, laboratories, lounges, offices, suites, based upon a contribution to the University.

B. Production Standards
- Database is maintained by Institutional Advancement of multiple other spaces and programs to assure a comprehensive resource list.

- Database is available on IA Intranet for access by staff.

- Database is reviewed annually with Facilities Management and Office of Provost.

C. Procedures
- Staff will have the ability to access the database for information such as, but not limited to: school, building, floor and room, type of room, gift amount, currently named, name, and date.

9. NAME REMOVAL OF FACILITIES AND PROGRAMS

A. Purpose

The purpose of this section is to assist staff in the removal of a named facility or program.

B. Production Standards

- Terminology on the removal of plaques will be included in all agreements.

- Name is removed when the donor fails to follow through on a commitment via a signed/executed gift agreement.

- Name is removed when a donor fails to maintain the high standards of the institution. (Donor is involved in a controversial situation such as a scandal, criminal or ethical problem that may cause embarrassment to the University.)

- Name is removed if the facility is being demolished or moved to another location.

- Name is removed if the gift was time-limited (period equal to the useful life of the facility or program).

- Approval on a case by case basis.

C. Procedures

- Development staff member contacts the Department of Operations and Quality Administration/ Director of Operations with the status of the pledge.

- The Department of Operations and Quality Administration / Director of Operations submits to the Vice Chancellor, Institutional Advancement/ Vice Chancellor, Health Sciences Development.

- The appropriate Vice Chancellor submits to the Provost/Senior Vice Chancellor for the Health Sciences.

Drafted: 10/10/06
Revised: 7/17/07

10. SIGNAGE

A. Purpose

The purpose of signage (plaques/donor walls) is to provide a vehicle through which the University can publicly express appreciation of the construction or renovation of a named facility while providing consistency throughout the University.

B. Production Standards

- Signage is reviewed and approved by the University Architects.

- Signage follows the architecture of the building.

- Signage for each building is standard and consistent.

C. Procedures

- Development staff member submits a request to University architects.

- University architect designs plaque.

Drafted: 10/10/06
Revised: 7/17/07

NAMED FACILITIES AND PROGRAMS OPPORTUNITY REQUEST FORM

Name of Originator (Development Staff)	Phone Number	E-mail Address

School/Department/Division

Facility or Program to be Named	Proposed Amount of Gift

Outright Gift _____ Pledge _____ *(Check one)*

Building	Floor	Room Number

Name of Donor(s)	Advance Entity ID Number(s)

Type of Gift: _____ Plant Fund in Facilities _____ Endowment Fund _____ Current Fund
(Check one. If both, enter amount of gift for each type.)

Type of Naming: _____ Time Limited _____ Perpetuity   :

Type of Facility/Program: _____ Existing Facility – Not Renovated or Renovation Complete
(Check one) _____ Existing Facility – To be Renovated
_____ New Facility
_____ New or Existing Program

Approvals:

Dean	Date

Vice Chancellor for Institutional Advancement/ Vice Chancellor for Health Sciences Development	Date

Provost/Senior Vice Chancellor for the Health Sciences	Date

Executive Vice Chancellor	Date

Chancellor (When required by Board of Trustees)	Date

Submit to Cynthia L. Roth, Associate Vice Chancellor, Operations and Quality Administration, 520 Craig Hall or email to Cynthia.Roth@ia.pitt.edu or Tom Spanedda, Director of Operations, Medical and Health Sciences Foundation, 400 Medical Arts Building or email to stom@pmhsf.org

UNIVERSITY OF WASHINGTON: FACILITIES AND SPACES NAMING POLICY (CAMPAIGN UNIVERSITY OF WASHINGTON: CREATING FUTURES FACILITIES AND SPACES NAMING POLICY)

General Policy

A building, outdoor area, and interior feature, object or space may be named for a person or family associated with the University community who has rendered distinguished service to the University or who has made a significant contribution to society. The above may also be named in recognition of a benefactor of the University who makes a significant contribution toward total project cost. In lieu of naming a building or area for the benefactor, the donor may propose that another person be honored in this manner, subject to the concurrence of the University.

Corporations or organizations are encouraged to be major benefactors of the University by recognizing a person or family important to their success. An interior feature, object or space may also be named for a corporation or organization. Only in rare situations will a building or outdoor area be named for

---

a corporation or organization whose gift represents a major contribution toward total project cost.

The President has final approval for naming interior features, objects and spaces. Final decision to name buildings and outdoor areas rests with the Board of Regents, upon recommendation of the President.

Naming actions shall not detract from the institution's values, dignity, integrity, or reputation, nor shall any such action create a conflict of interest or confer special privileges.

Individual/Family Naming Guidelines

A. Buildings or Outdoor Areas A building or outdoor area may be named for a person or family associated with the University community who has rendered distinguished service to the University or who has made a significant contribution to society. The above also may be named as agreed to with a benefactor of the University whose gifts represent a significant contribution toward the project cost, based upon the following criteria.

1. The individual has a prominent relationship with the University and/or the region, and he or she has a positive image and demonstrated integrity. In the event of changed circumstances, the University reserves the right, on reasonable grounds, to revise the form of or withdraw recognition in consultation with the donor when possible.

2. The guidelines for determining the gift amount that represents "a significant contribution" to the project cost are as follows:

   a. While a minimum of 50% of the project cost (which may include an operating endowment) is the desired amount for naming, the target gift amount for naming will be set for each project as part of the Business Plan section (see attached) of the Project Agreement.

   b. Donations for naming should be realized in full within five years of the commitment.

     1. Buildings named for an individual or family generally will be termed "____ Hall." If a functional title is selected, the building may be named "____ Building."

     2. The name will remain on the building or outdoor area for the life of the building or area (subject to Section 2A1). If at some future time the building or area is replaced (which may include a major reconstruction that substantially changes the functions/appearance of a building's interior and exterior), the name may or may not be carried on the replacement facility as approved by the Board of Regents. If the name is not used on the replacement facility, the Board of Regents will determine the appropriate recognition to be incorporated into the new building or area.

B. Interior Features, Objects or Spaces   A named interior feature, object or space will not be exhibited on external building walls; the name will be located as close as possible to (and otherwise affiliated with) the funded feature, object or space.

An interior feature, object or space may be named for a person or family associated with the University community who has rendered distinguished service to the University or who has made a significant contribution to society. The above also may be named as agreed to with a benefactor of the University whose gifts represent a significant contribution toward the project cost or the purchase of the object, based upon the following criteria.

1. The individual has a prominent relationship with the University and/or the region, and he or she has a positive image and demonstrated integrity. In the event of changed circumstances, the University reserves the right, on reasonable grounds, to revise the form of or withdraw recognition in consultation with the donor when possible.

2. The guidelines for determining the gift amount that represents "a significant contribution" to the project cost are as follows:

   a. While the desired goal for a naming gift is the cost to provide and equip the space (which may include an operating endowment), the target gift amount for naming will be set for each project in advance of soliciting donors in coordination with the Vice President for Development and Alumni Relations. Interior spaces that are part of a total building fundraising campaign should be included as part of the Business Plan section (see attached) of the Project Agreement.

b. Donations for naming should be realized in full within five years of the commitment.

1. The name will remain for the life of the feature, object or space with appropriate recognition as determined by the President if it is replaced.

Corporate/Organizational Naming Guidelines

A. Buildings or Outdoor Areas   Corporations or organizations are encouraged to be major benefactors of the University by recognizing a person or family important to their success. Only in rare situations will a building or outdoor area be named for a corporation or organization whose gifts represent a significant contribution toward the project cost, based upon the following criteria.

1. The corporation or organization has a prominent relationship with the University and/or the region, and it has a positive image and demonstrated integrity. In the event of changed circumstances, the University

reserves the right, on reasonable grounds, to revise the form of or withdraw recognition in consultation with the donor when possible.

2. The guidelines for determining the gift amount that represents "a significant contribution" to the project cost are as follows:

a. A minimum of 50% of the project cost (which may include an operating endowment) is provided unless a different gift amount for naming is specified as part of the Business Plan section (see attached) of the Project Agreement.

b. Donations for naming should be realized in full within five years of the commitment.

1. Buildings named for a corporation or organization generally will be termed "___ Hall." If a functional title is selected, the building may be named "___ Building."

2. In cases where the entity name is used, the gift agreement will specify the number of years during which the building or area will be named. It will include the clause that any name changes during that period will be at the University's sole discretion, subject to approval by the Board of Regents.

B. Interior Features, Objects or Spaces　A named interior feature, object or space will not be exhibited on external building walls; the name will be located as close as possible to (and otherwise affiliated with) the funded feature, object or space.

An interior feature, object or space may be named for a corporation or organization whose gifts represent a significant contribution toward the project cost or the purchase of the object, based upon the following criteria.

1. The corporation/organization has a prominent relationship with the University and/or the region, and it has a positive image and demonstrated integrity. In the event of changed circumstances, the University reserves the right, on reasonable grounds, to revise the form of or withdraw recognition in consultation with the donor when possible.

2. The guidelines for determining the gift amount that represents "a significant contribution" to the project cost are as follows:

   a. While the desired goal for a naming gift is the cost to provide and equip the space (which may include an operating endowment), the target gift amount for naming will be set for each project in advance of soliciting donors in coordination with the Vice President for Development and Alumni Relations. Interior spaces that are part of a total building fundraising campaign should be included as part of the Business Plan section (see attached) of the Project Agreement. Donations for naming should be realized in full within five years of the commitment.

1. In cases where the entity name is used, the gift agreement will specify the number of years during which the feature, object or space will be named, and it will include the clause that any name changes during that period will be at the University's sole discretion, subject to approval by the President.

Approval Process

Proposals for naming opportunities will follow the approval process described below in order to obtain appropriate approvals before publicly discussing recognition of a person, family, corporation or organization and before approaching a prospective donor for a naming gift.

Each campus of the University of Washington, UW Bothell, UW Seattle, and UW Tacoma, is responsible for developing campus-specific processes and committees for approval for the naming of facilities, including but not limited to buildings, outdoor areas, interior features, objects or spaces at their respective campuses. The UW Bothell and UW Tacoma will forward their recommendations through the Chancellors to the President. The UW Seattle will forward its recommendations from the UW Seattle Names Committee to the President.

Members of the Names Committees at the three campuses will advise proposers on the respective campuses to ensure that the naming decisions reflect University of Washington values.

The President has final approval for naming interior features, objects and spaces. Final decision to name buildings and outdoor areas rests with the Board of Regents, upon recommendation of the President.

A. Recognition of Distinguished Service

1. The Dean, Vice President, Director of Libraries or Director of Athletics will prepare and submit a recommendation for naming to the appropriate Names Committee, along with background materials for consideration.

2. That Names Committee (or Chancellor) will forward favorable recommendations to the President. If approved, the President will forward the naming request to the Board of Regents, which has the authority to make the final decision on naming buildings or outdoor areas, or if it relates to an interior feature, object or space, notify the appropriate Names Committee (or Chancellor) of the approval.

B. *Recognition of a Benefactor: Buildings or Outdoor Areas*

1. The Dean, Chancellor, Vice President, Director of Libraries or Director of Athletics will review the suggested project scope, business plan, and donor potential with the Provost. If the proposal is accepted, the Provost will initiate the development of a Project Agreement to verify the project cost estimates with the project scope, business plan (including operating and maintenance costs, as well as any surge space needs), and donor potentials, along with project milestones. The appropriate Names Committee (or Chancellor) will be consulted as part of the development of the Project Agreement, prior to bringing a specific naming request for their approval.

2. The Project Agreement approvals include the Provost, appropriate Chancellor, Dean or Vice President, Vice President for Development and Alumni Relations, and Executive Vice President. The President and Regents will be advised about Project Agreements during the approval process.

3. Once a Project Agreement has been approved, plans for the fundraising campaign will be initiated and fundraising contacts are authorized to begin.

4. When a naming donor has been identified, the Chancellor, Dean, Vice President, Director

of Libraries or Director of Athletics will prepare and submit a recommendation for naming to the appropriate Names Committee, along with background materials for consideration. The Names Committee (or Chancellor) will forward favorable recommendations to the President. If approved, the President will forward the naming request to the Board of Regents, which has the authority to make the final decision on naming buildings.

5. Project pre-design, design and construction activities will be initiated when the fundraising amounts specified in the approved Project Agreement have been achieved.

C. Recognition of a Benefactor: Interior Features, Objects or Spaces

1. If the interior feature, object or space is part of a larger fundraising effort, e.g., a new building, the process above will be followed, utilizing the Project Agreement.

   a. If the interior feature, object or space is a stand-alone item, the Chancellor, Dean, Vice President, Director of Libraries or Director of Athletics will prepare and submit a recommendation for naming to the appropriate Names Committee, along with background materials for consideration. The Names Committee (or Chancellor) will forward favorable recommendations to the President for approval.

CAMPAIGN UNIVERSITY OF WASHINGTON: CREATING FUTURES ENDOWMENT AND PROGRAM NAMING POLICY

I. Introduction

Significant gifts to support the University of Washington offer an opportunity to appropriately recognize donors. This recognition may include the creation of permanently named endowment funds and/or named programs.

An endowment is a permanent fund established for a specific purpose. The principal of an endowed fund is invested to grow over time while the distributions it produces are used to support the endowment's purpose. Gifts for endowment are extremely valuable in enhancing the quality of the University of Washington's teaching, research, facilities and student experience, since endowments provide perpetual funding for their intended purpose. They need to be regularly expended, and donors need to be acknowledged on a regular (at least annual) basis.

Because of their permanent nature, named endowments must be established with great care and sensitivity to the goals and needs of both the donors and the University. The suggested minimum may vary by college or discipline and may also be adjusted from time to time in proportion to changing costs. The University reserves the right to make final determinations in specific cases.

The endowment agreement (a document signed by the donors and appropriate academic and administrative leadership) drafted for a particular gift outlines the use and administration of that gift. Endowment gifts shall be invested in the Consolidated Endowment Fund (CEF) administered by the University. The investment, management and expenditure of funds shall be in accordance with University policies and procedures.

The purposes of these naming criteria are to:

- provide guidance to prospective donors and to University staff about the desired size of a gift to attain a particular naming opportunity.
- promote uniform naming levels in all UW schools, colleges, programs and campuses.
- ensure that permanent endowments are at sufficiently high levels to appropriately support the desired purposes.
- provide a mechanism for evaluating proposed major naming gifts through the appropriate channels.

II. Types of Endowed Support

A. Endowed Funds   Endowed funds offer donors the opportunity to give the University and departments maximum flexibility in enhancing their respective programs. Purposes for these funds may include: unrestricted or broadly-defined support, library collections, student travel, publications series, etc.

The minimum outright gift for support is as follows:

• Endowed Fund $25,000 and above

1. Administration   Endowed funds are available for use by the designated unit. The appropriate administrative or academic leader shall be responsible for administering expenditures from the fund, consistent with the stated uses as defined in the endowment agreement.

B. *Scholarships and Fellowships*   Endowed scholarships and fellowships offer donors the opportunity to make possible a university education for deserving students. Endowment agreements provide the vehicle for identifying the criteria by which students are selected.

Donors do not directly participate in the selection process, but will be notified of the selection.

The minimum outright gifts for various levels of student support are as follows:

Undergraduate Student Support:

• Scholarship $ 50,000 and above
• Presidential Scholarship $100,000 and above
• Regental Scholarship $250,000 and above

Graduate Student Support:

• Fellowship $100,000 and above

- Presidential Fellowship $250,000 and above
- Regental Fellowship $500,000 and above

1. Appointments and Criteria   The selection of scholarship and fellowship recipients should be consistent with donor intent as articulated in the endowment agreement. In determining the language for these agreements, the selection criteria should reflect information about students that is readily available from University records.

2. Administration   University-wide scholarships shall be approved and signed by the Vice President for Student Affairs. University-wide fellowships shall be approved and signed by the Dean of the Graduate School. Chancellors, Deans and Vice Presidents shall approve and sign unit-based scholarship and fellowship endowment agreements pertinent to their areas. The University official signing the agreement is responsible for ensuring that the expenditures are consistent with the endowment agreement.

C. Endowed Staff Positions   Named positions endowed through private gifts provide creative and on-going support for roles that are not necessarily academically based but are important to the University's academic mission. Positions that can be endowed include, but are not limited to, curators, librarians, directors and archivists.

The minimum outright gift for endowed staff support is as follows:

• Endowed Staff Position $250,000 and above

1. Appointments and Criteria   The appointment of recipients should be consistent with donor intent as articulated in the endowment agreement. In determining these agreements, the terms should reflect general operating practices of the University and outline alternative uses in case positions change over time.

2. Administration   Deans, Chancellors and the Director of University Libraries shall be responsible for administering expenditures related to unit positions in accordance with University policies and procedures and for ensuring that expenditures are consistent with the endowment agreement approved by the donor.

D. Chairs, Professorships and Fellowships   The University of Washington seeks support for the creation of endowed chairs and professorships, which provide significant benefits in recruiting and retaining outstanding faculty at the University. These endowed gifts greatly enrich support for the teaching and research activities of distinguished faculty and bring public recognition of their status.

Both chairs and professorships may be used to supplement the base salaries of faculty members.

They also may provide professional support for the activities of faculty members appointed to the endowed position, including, but not restricted to, research assistance, travel and staff support.

The minimum outright gifts for various levels of faculty support are as follows:

- Faculty Fellowship $ 100,000 and above
- Professorship $ 250,000 and above
- Chair $1,000,000 and above
- Regental Chair $3,000,000 and above

In addition, the University offers an opportunity to support faculty via a non-endowed vehicle:

- Professorship (Term) $15,000 and above/year for 3-5 years

1. Appointments and Criteria   The Regents of the University of Washington have delegated the authority to establish named endowed professorships and chairs to the Vice President for Development and Alumni Relations, unless there is something unusual or special about the gift that would benefit from regental review.

Appointments to professorships and chairs involve appropriate levels of faculty advice. The appropriate Chancellor or Dean shall recommend a candidate to the Provost, who shall in turn recommend the candidate to the President for approval by the Regents.

Donors do not directly participate in the selection process, but in the endowment agreement they may specify an academic area where the endowment should be focused. Donors will be notified of the appointment.

Depending on the wishes of the donor and the concurrence of the appropriate Chancellor or Dean and the Provost, a professorship or chair may be filled by a recipient for an indefinite period, subject to review at least every five years, or it may be a rotating professorship or chair for a shorter period of time.

The President shall assign university-wide professorships and chairs to the various academic disciplines and units at his/her discretion.

2. Administration   Chancellors and Deans shall be responsible for administering expenditures related to endowed professorships and chairs in accordance with University policies and procedures to assure that administration is consistent with the endowment agreement.

The designated field for an endowed professorship or chair may be specified to include academic departments and major sub-disciplines within a department, school or college.

Distributions from the endowment shall support positions within the academic discipline specified by the donor at the time of acceptance of the gift so long as that discipline or area of study continues at the University. The endowment agreement shall permit appropriate alternative use of the

distributions by the Regents, upon the recommendation of the President, should the subject area of
the professorship or chair cease to be consistent with
the University's mission or its academic plan. Such
alternative distribution shall be as closely related to
the donor's original intent as is feasible.

In years when a professorship or chair is vacant,
the administrator, as provided in the endowment
agreement, may elect to a) return the endowment's
annual distributions to the principal or b) desig-
nate the distributions for support of faculty and/or
students in the field supported by the endowment.

E. Schools, Colleges and Programs   For gift-related
naming opportunities, endowing a school, college
or program offers donors a premier opportunity to
substantially benefit a particular unit of the University. Because naming represents an important
event in the history of the institution, it requires
an extraordinary gift. The endowment should gen-
erate a distribution that provides significant support to the annual operating budget of the entity
named.

1. Administration   All naming actions shall be
by action of the Board of Regents upon recommendation of the President.

In naming a school, college or program, the
Regents, University President, Provost, and other
administrators and development staff must be
involved prior to reaching final agreement with a
donor. (For naming of facilities, refer to the "Facilities and Spaces Naming Policy.")

Naming actions shall not detract from the institution's values, dignity, integrity, or reputation, nor shall any such action create a conflict of interest or confer special privileges. In the event of changed circumstances, the University reserves the right, on reasonable grounds, to revise the form of or withdraw recognition in consultation with the donor when possible.

HISTORIC NAMED GIFT
SURVEY FORM

The information gathering process is an important part of developing your inventory of properties. Add additional rows as needed. Start by conducting a survey of what has been named in the past using a data collection table like the one below:

Named Building and Outdoor Space	Name of Donor	What Year	Dollar Amount

Index